THE WIND IN THE RIGGING

THE
WIND
IN THE
RIGGING

CAPTAIN JACK DODD

BOULDER
PUBLICATIONS

LIBRARY AND ARCHIVES CANADA CATALOGUING IN PUBLICATION

Dodd, Jack, 1902-1978
 Wind in the rigging / Jack Dodd.

Originally published: Torbay, N.L. : J. Dodd, 1972.
ISBN 978-1-927099-14-8

 1. Dodd, Jack, 1902-1978. 2. Sailors--Newfoundland and
Labrador--Biography. 3. Seafaring life. 4. Voyages and travels. I. Title.

G540.D56 2012   910.4'5   C2012-906218-9

We acknowledge the financial support of the Government of
Newfoundland and Labrador through the Department of
Tourism, Culture and Recreation.

We acknowledge the financial support for our publishing
program by the Government of Canada and the Department
of Canadian Heritage through the Canada Book Fund.

Published by Boulder Publications
Portugal Cove-St. Philip's, Newfoundland and Labrador
www.boulderpublications.ca

Copy editor: Iona Bulgin
Cover design and layout: Alison Carr

Printed in Canada

ABOUT JACK DODD

Jack Dodd was born on June 2, 1902, in Torbay, Newfoundland and Labrador. His parents, William and Lucille (Crowe) Dodd, made a good living from fishing and farming. At an early age Dodd joined his father on the fishing boat.

Dodd attended Holy Trinity School in Torbay, receiving a grade 7 education before turning his attention fully to a life on the water.

As a seaman, Dodd voyaged around the world three times, through the Panama Canal nine times, and around Cape Horn nine times. Along the way, he was shipwrecked at least seven times and had dozens of other close calls.

Dodd eventually retired from his seafaring ways but would be called "Captain" for the rest of his life—a mark of respect for his years at sea. He then turned his attention to prospecting for gold and other minerals in the United States and Canada—a January 1964 article in *St. John's Woman* credits him as being the discoverer of uranium in Newfoundland.

St. John's Woman also published a series of adventure stories that year written by Cassie Brown from her interviews with Dodd. It also featured an article ("Author known!," January 1964) detailing Dodd's claim that he wrote the traditional folksong "The Star of Logy Bay." Dodd's original lyrics are included in *The Wind in the Rigging*.

In his later, landlocked, years, Dodd's name became familiar to many in Newfoundland as an advocate and letter writer. His frequent letters to the editor, many about the state of the province's fisheries, were published in the St. John's *Evening Telegram*, the *Daily News*, and *The Newfoundland Herald*; government officials and radio listeners also received regular commentary and advice from Dodd.

Dodd self-published two books: *The Wind in the Rigging* (1972) and *Cabot's Voyage to Newfoundland* (1974). The latter tells the story of John Cabot's voyage to Newfoundland and his alleged landfall in Flat Rock in 1497.

Dodd was also known locally for his weather predictions. For "Capt. Jack Dodd—Fisherman, flag designer, book writer, and Newfoundland's weather prophet," an article published in *The Newfoundland Herald*, December 28, 1977, writer Paul Sparkes contacted Dodd, not for the first time, for a weather report for the year ahead. Sparkes concluded his article: "He might be weather-beaten by years on the briny deep, but he doesn't change. Captain Jack Dodd, formerly of Torbay and now of Harbour Grace, he's an entertainment medium in himself!"

Jack Dodd died in 1978.

This edition of *The Wind in the Rigging* is based on the original edition self-published by Dodd in 1972; spelling has been standardized and modernized, inconsistencies corrected, and some light editing done to ensure clarity and readability.

CHAPTER 1

Newfoundland is Britain's oldest colony. It was discovered by John Cabot on June 24, 1497. St. John's is the oldest city in North America. It was first settled in the early part of the fifteenth century, long before the Pilgrims landed at Plymouth, Massachusetts, where today the famous Plymouth Rock stands as a symbol to the American Pilgrim Fathers.

St. John's is located on the east coast of Newfoundland. Torbay is the nearest outport settlement. It is 7 miles to the north of the capital city of St. John's. In these two places Newfoundland's history began, and down through the years it has been a most blustery history, to say the least.

The island is noted for its fishery, mineral resources, and salmon rivers, which makes it a sportsman's paradise.

It was in Torbay, just after the turn of the century, on June 2, 1902, that I was born. My father, William Dodd, was a commercial fisherman, who married the daughter of Richard Crowe, who was a farmer. This farm was located in Rainbow Valley in Torbay.

As the time drew near for my birth, my father was in the middle of the fishery, and someone had to look after my mother. My grandfather told my father to continue fishing and he would look after her and see that the nurse, usually a midwife, was obtainable. There were no doctors at this time in Torbay, and the midwife delivered all the children.

When the time came for me to be born, my grandfather brought the midwife by horse team. She was a woman up in her seventies with grey hair and was dressed in long skirts. My grandmother at this time was very active and all excited about the event. Some other local ladies came to help. One of these, Granny Dawson, smoked a clay pipe and had two snuff boxes, one with fine snuff, the other with coarse. These women made quite a picture with their dresses touching the floor.

Birthplace of Jack Dodd, Rainbow Valley, Torbay.

The children, then ranging from five to ten years, were sent from the house. My grandmother saw to all of this. This was in the days when children were supposed to be seen and not heard! When I was born, the midwife brought me downstairs and laid me on blankets on the kitchen table, where I was first bathed and clothed; then the children were allowed to return to the house. My sisters and brothers began asking questions of the midwife.

The oldest said, "Nurse, is it a boy or girl?" She answered, "It is a boy and born with a caul." One of the girls asked what this meant and the midwife explained that the child could be a priest, doctor, captain, and so on—someone with a call to active duty. She went on, "What he really will be is a great sailor. He is going to sail the seven seas and visit more ports of the world than any other Torbay man has ever done." I was to find out that this prediction laid down by the nurse came true in the days ahead.

The old stove in the farmhouse where Jack was born.

My mother remained with her family while my father was building a new home in Torbay. This was farther out by the harbour, and it seemed from the start that my life began with strange happenings, which were to follow me the rest of my days. The first one happened when I was three months old. My mother went to St. John's, 7 miles away, to do some shopping. It was during haymaking time and, also, a very busy time in the fishery. She left my father babysitting and she thought he would stay at my grandfather's. However, after she went to town, my father decided to go down to his hayfield and do some mowing. He took me along with him and laid me down in the field while he went along with his mowing. While my father was mowing the hay in the field, his fishing partner called him from the road and told him to come along—they were starting to catch squid out in the harbour. My father told him he couldn't go, as he had to look after the baby.

His partner said, "Take him with you," and this is what my father did. I took my first sea trip at the age of three months!

They took me to where the whale boat was moored on the squid-jigging ground and laid me on the deck of the whale boat (which was midship). The two of them started catching squid, and it wasn't long before squid juice was flying all over the boat. Finally, my father looked around at me and said, "Chris, look at the state of the baby." I was in some mess, with black squid juice all over me.

Chris said, "That's his first baptism of the sea," adding, "Don't worry about the baby; I'll have him cleaned up in a minute." He took the deck mop and dipped it overboard and washed me with salt water.

My father took me home and, without changing any of my clothing, put me in my cradle. When my mother arrived several hours later and saw the condition I was in, with the squid juice and salt water on my clothes, she asked my father, "What happened to the baby?"

He said, "I had him out on the squid-jigging ground."

The cradle I was kept in was made by a fellow who used to visit the homestead. His name was William Browne and he was lost in the *Greenland* sealing disaster. The cradle was constructed of oak and had a hood over it and two rockers.

As I grew up, things were pretty lively around the farmhouse. One of my aunts played an accordion and kitchen dances were in full swing! We would have an elderly blind man come to play the fiddle and he would sit on a chair in the corner of the house. Putting him in the corner of the house would give him protection from the fighting which would take place before the dancing was over. The dancing included quadrilles, reels, lancers, square dancing, and waltzes, and two or three old ladies out doing the horn pipe.

Granny Dawson rocking baby Jack Dodd while
knitting and smoking a clay pipe.

If the fiddler was late getting to the dance, it still would start on time because the ladies would begin to sing and the people would go on with the dances.

I would like to say something about my grandfather, who was decorated three times for bravery in life-saving. His performance in these matters was really outstanding but, as with many other Newfoundlanders, his praises were very little mentioned. On one occasion he saved the lives of 20 people from two schooners in Torbay Harbour. The schooners were anchored in the harbour, and the seas around the land were so rough it was impossible to launch a boat. My grandfather, who was a strong swimmer, tied a heavy fishing line around his waist and swam out to one of the schooners. This was in the early part of December, on a freezing day with heavy snow showers. A breeches buoy was rigged from the vessels to the shore. For this he received a medal for life-saving.

In March, 1891, while he was searching for seals off Torbay with seven other companions, the ice broke off midway across the bay, trapping all eight men on the outside floe. He tied a sealing rope around his waist and had all the other men join the ropes fast to this one. Then he took off his clothing, rolled it up, and tied it around his shoulders.

My grandfather plunged into the cold water and swam across to the main ice, landing on the other side of the ice. Without putting on his clothes and standing there in the cold northwest wind and snow, he pulled all of his seven companions to safety (on the ice that was still connected to the land). For this, he received a gold medal from the governor of Newfoundland. When the governor presented him with the medal, he had this to say: "I can't call you a man for what you have done. You are a Newfoundland dog."

The other act of bravery was when he launched a boat at Tapper's Cove and saved people's lives in a shipwreck. One of the medals awarded him was gold and today it would be worth a lot of money. I was in for a big surprise in later years when I asked the family what had become of my grandfather's medals. I was told they were put in the casket and today these valuable medals are buried with him in the cemetery in Torbay. Yes, I feel very proud of my grandfather, who was a wonderful man, kind and very popular with government officials in the city.

I was three years old when we moved to a new home down at the Torbay waterfront, but I made many visits to my grandfather's farm-house and learned from him quite a bit of woodcraft, because in my younger days I was very active in hunting and ranging in the forest.

I attended school at Torbay, where I was more interested in learning navigation than any other subject. At this time Augustus Thorne was the teacher at Torbay. He later became a priest and was stationed at Lamaline and St. Lawrence on the Burin Peninsula, where he stayed until his death. Then I had a well-known schoolmaster by the name of Leo English, who afterwards became a museum head and a historian. From him, I learned quite a bit of navigation. He was a navigation teacher, yet he never went to sea!

When I was attending school, Torbay was a thriving fishing community with 110 commercial boats and equipment. The flakes and stages were so close together that there was no room for any more on the north side of Torbay and the west end of the harbour. There were three government docks in the harbour and cook shacks were scattered all over the place.

The stage is a fisherman's stage. It is built on the side of the sea and constructed of different types of wood brought out of the nearby forest. The stage is put up on stilts. The roof is sometimes covered with tree bark, called rinds by the fishermen. The fish is taken ashore from the boat, processed on the table in this stage, and put into large boxes and salted. It stays in salt for about 10 days. Then it is taken out and placed on the flakes to be dried in the wind and sun.

The flake is built out of the same material as the stage, with rails stowed thickly together so that you can walk on them. The flake is then coated over with spruce boughs and the fish is placed on them to dry in the sun.

Most of the fishing boats were rowed or sailed until 1910, when the first motorboats came to Torbay. The women of the harbour handled most of the dried fish. It was quite a sight to see the women in the morning, wearing their large white aprons, spreading the fish on the flake, and in the evening it was the same performance. It was common to see two women carrying a barrow-tub of fresh fish or a hand barrow of dried fish! Most of the cooking, normally done by the women, was performed in large cookhouses.

The sounds of cowbells (cows were all over the place), the convent bell that used to ring at noon and 5 p.m., and the Anglican church bell were very familiar in my boyhood days. All this is now gone and lives only in my memory.

Fishing was a very rugged life and a hard way to make a livelihood. It was hard work from daylight until dark and, on some occasions, one had to work through the night without getting any rest. The fishermen of Newfoundland were about the hardest working people in the world, but this has all changed now and fishing is more of a sports event than anything else. The young men who are growing up seem to get an education, which their forefathers did not have. Then they get an office job, a nice car, and a nice girlfriend; they work from 9 a.m. until 4:30 p.m.; and then they visit the beer parlours and have a good time. Yes, it's quite a change since my boyhood in Newfoundland.

I was about 16 years old when first I took part in cod-trap fishing. This was roughly in 1919 after the First World War. This trap berth I am telling about is located at a place on the north side of Torbay called Gull Rock. The trap was owned by Patrick Thorne, who was nicknamed Thunder. He was a skilled fisherman and always liked to fish at Gull Rock. On the evening of June 28, 1919, we had one of the biggest hauls of codfish ever hauled in any Newfoundland trap—400 quintals (or 88,184 pounds).

On this occasion he gave away 225 quintals to the fishermen of Torbay and salted for himself on shore 175 quintals. This was a record haul and I feel proud to have taken part in the same.

The *Newfoundland* Disaster of 1914

I saw the SS *Bellaventure* on the morning she arrived in the Narrows of St. John's with some 80 frozen bodies of seal hunters. It was very sad, indeed, to see people from many outports gathering around the waterfront in order to claim the bodies of their loved ones.

The bodies were mostly placed in white pine boxes; many of the coffins were hauled by horses on sleighs along Torbay Road. Quite a few went to Pouch Cove and different places around the bay.

In later years I was shipmates with one of the survivors, who told me the story of what had taken place on the ice. This is his account: The captain of the SS *Stephano*, whose name was Abram Kean, and the captain of the sealer SS *Newfoundland* were father and son. The man, Jim, who told me the story, was a seal hunter on the *Newfoundland*. The *Newfoundland* was jammed in the ice but the *Stephano* was free and could move in any direction. The captain of the *Stephano* took some of the *Newfoundland* men (about 130) aboard the *Stephano* to take them to a seal patch, but it seemed as if the plan did not materialize. Then he sent the men on foot to travel back to the *Newfoundland*. Some of the men refused to leave the *Stephano* as they thought a storm was coming up and they wouldn't be able to make it. However, the captain of the *Stephano* would not let them stay on board his ship—they were forced to go by foot! While they were travelling back to their ship, they were overtaken by a severe blizzard. The snow was so thick that most of the men strayed from one another.

Jim found himself with seven companions in the blizzard, and they tried to get shelter from heavy pinnacles of ice that surrounded a large ice pan. They tried to keep themselves warm by dancing around the pan. A man by the name of Jordon from Pouch Cove sat on a lump of ice and was singing for a group of men to dance; he stumbled off the lump of ice and, to their surprise, he was dead! The other men hauled his body to one side of the ice pan. It was not long before another man dropped dead. Jim saw all seven of his companions die on that ice pan. This was the first night of the blizzard. After all seven men died on the pan, he left it with the dead and wandered out into the storm. He was going in search of someone alive.

Jim hadn't gone far after leaving the pan when he fell through the ice. He went down to his shoulders before he caught another pan to keep him up. He never dreamed he would get out of the water again, but with the help of his gaff he managed to get onto the ice. Thoroughly wet and in freezing temperatures, Jim thought it was the end. He struggled along in the thick drifts of snow until he came to two big lumps of ice that looked like boulders. He crawled behind these for some shelter, and he discovered eight frozen bodies on the pan! Jim noticed that one of the dead men's clothes were dry. After looking over the man with the dry clothes, a thought came to him. He knew he could not live long himself with frozen clothes on and he knew that dry clothes were no good to the dead man; so he took the clothes off the dead body and changed into them. This saved his life.

After doing this, Jim left the pan with the other dead bodies and wandered out into the storm again. In a short while he got to a big pan of ice where there were 50 or 60 men. Quite a few of these men were already dead, but that is where Jim spent the second night out in the storm. Over 50 men died on this pan, and he lived.

Jim Evoy survived the *Newfoundland* disaster, suffering only two frostbitten toes. He was one of the toughest and bravest men to be found anywhere on the island of Newfoundland.

About the time that the dead were brought into St. John's the SS *Southern Cross* left the Gulf on Newfoundland's West Coast with a full load of young harp seals to come to St. John's. The *Southern Cross* disappeared with all hands, and not one piece of wreckage or any of the crew's belongings were ever found. She carried a crew of 130 men. This was a very sad happening for the wives and mothers and loved ones who were left to mourn their loss.

There was one man who is outstanding in my memory: Patrick Keats. He made 19 trips in the *Southern Cross*, and most of the trips were full loads of seals, but in the spring of 1914 a funny thing happened to Pat. He went to sign on with the ship, and when he arrived at the office he found it was crowded. He thought he would leave and return in the afternoon. Pat liked a drink and most times had a flask in his pocket. He had a pint of rum this morning and after leaving Baine Johnston's office, he walked down to the pier where the *Southern Cross* was tied up. Standing by the shed, he took out his pint of rum and had a drink. He thought he saw something come down from the ship and, as it arrived on the dock, Pat's eyes spread with surprise. It was a rat leaving the ship, followed by four or five more.

Pat took another drink from his flask and then went back to the office, where he gave up the number of his berth. When he passed his number to the office man, he said, "I won't be going." When the office man asked why, Pat told him, "I don't feel so good, and I don't think I'll make the voyage this spring."

After leaving the office and returning to the street, he met two of his crewmen. After relating the story of the rats leaving the ship, he advised them not to go on the *Southern Cross*. But they only laughed at him and said it was just superstition. Those two poor fellows went out on the ship.

Seeing rats leaving a ship is not cause for superstition, for down through the years it has been conceded that this ship was lost. But not everyone sees rats leaving a ship and, in Pat's case, he was lucky, for the rats saved his life!

After the *Southern Cross* arrived in the Gulf and obtained her full load of seals, Pat's friends in Torbay began to laugh at his superstition. One fellow said to him, "The *Southern Cross* is on her way home with a load of seals and you'll lose a good bill this spring by not going there."

His answer was, "She has not reached port yet." And Pat was right! The *Southern Cross* never reached St. John's, and nothing was ever heard of her again.

At an early age I started fishing in Torbay with my father, who was a successful fisherman and well acquainted with the fishing grounds. From him I learned quite a lot about the fishing business, which was in full swing at that time in the Torbay area.

There were some boats under sail, some of which were called jack boats. A jack is a small schooner with two masts. It has a mainsail, foresail, jumbo, and jib. At this time they were fast dying out, and the fishermen were building trap skiffs. The trap skiff could be used for trap fishing, longlining, and also handlining. Handlining was done with a jigger or lead, hook, and bait. The so-called longliner that the government of Newfoundland has been talking about building is not new in Newfoundland. Longlining has been going on since John Cabot landed. It was called trawling.

A trawl is a 50-fathom line with a gangen and hook attached to the line with a 1-fathom space between each; then several 50-fathom lines could be joined together, making the trawl 50 to 800 fathoms long. This trawl is hauled from the boat, which could be a trap skiff or a dory. This type of fishing has been carried on down through Newfoundland history.

There is one outstanding fishing ground in this area—it is called Tantum Shoals. Fish can be found around this ground year-round. The shoal part of the bank has 2 fathoms of water and when the wind is east or southeast, the shoal breaks and the seas kicked by the winds roll onto Torbay Point, a mile away. It is very dangerous and precautions have to be taken by those who fish there. There are more fishing grounds along the east coast—Lily Bank, Codner, New Ground, the Beamor, White Sledge, and Robin, where codfish can be taken any time of the year.

Early fishermen had to row their boats to these places. It was hard work, and you had to be in good shape to carry it out.

While speaking of the east coast in the Torbay area, I would like to refer to the people of Cabot's time in Dublin, Ireland. There was one lady, Mrs. Mary Dawson, whom I used to visit very often in my young days. She was an Irishwoman, born in County Mayo, and she had a diary written by Dan McCarthy, who had spent a winter in Newfoundland and is supposed to have been the first settler in Torbay, and probably in Newfoundland. The diary was handed down to Mrs. Dawson and is dated back to the fifteenth century.

Granny Dawson, as I called her, could tell you all about Cabot, his boyhood days, when he went to the monastery in Italy, and when he left Italy and returned to England. His return to Italy occurred before he sailed on his voyage of discovery. According to the diary, Cabot landed on Flat Rock in Torbay and, after quite an investigation by me, I believe that she was right. She went on to tell me that in the early morning of June 24, 1497, one of Cabot's men was in the crow's nest. His name was O'Driscoll and, when relieved of his watch, he said to the man, "I am glad you came to relieve me. I am so exhausted that I am seeing red." After the other man took over the watch in the crow's nest, O'Driscoll had just reached the deck of the *Matthew*, when the man hollered out, "Land ahoy!" He was answered from the deck right away, and the man from the crow's nest said, "On your starboard side."

Red Head, Flat Rock, first land sighted by Cabot.

The land that Granny Dawson referred to is today called Red Head in Flat Rock and showed up red in the distance. So the man who said he was seeing red was actually looking at land. The landing was made in Flat Rock on the west side of Flat Rock Harbour by the river. On June 26, a small boat that the *Matthew* carried made the trip to Torbay, landing on a small beach on the other side of Torbay. John Cabot climbed up to the top of a large rock overlooking Torbay Harbour and looked down on the countryside, which was all wooded at the time. The rock is still called Cabot Rock and is situated on the north side of Torbay between Tapper's Cove and Treasure Cove.

It was at Treasure Cove that I dug up a stone embedded in mortar. After knocking off the covering of mortar, I was surprised to see scratchings on the rock. It was more than scratchings; it was cuttings: John Cabot's name, the name of the discovery ship, the *Matthew*, the date of the discovery, June 24, 1497, and what looked like a tiara (the Pope wears this on his head and it seemed to have some connection with the words written on the stone) were on the rock and many more cuttings. The stone itself is in the shape of a human foot and is not native to Newfoundland. This certainly agrees with the description of Cabot from the diary, and I am finally convinced that he landed in the vicinity of Torbay and not Cape Freels.

Flat Rock, northeast of St. John's,
where Jack Dodd believes Cabot first landed.

My first adventure and narrow escape with my life was in 1917. At this time the ice came into Torbay Harbour and filled the bay. My two companions and I left early in the morning to hunt for seals. We went about 5 miles from Torbay, but had no luck. Then we discovered the wind came from the west and the ice had broken off from the harbour ice, leaving the harbour packed with ice and us adrift on the outside floe. We could see that the ice seemed to be closer to the northern shore than it was to the southern shore, so we made our way, running and stumbling, to the north shore. When we got there, the ice was near the rocks; it was all chopped up and like slush. We tried several places to make a landing but were unsuccessful.

When we were close to the shore, we made our way across the broken ice with great difficulty and finally reached the rocks. All three of us managed to get ashore on a shelf of rock with a cliff 150 feet above us. We were on the land but in a bad predicament, for the tide at this time was low. When it rose, it would come in over the rock, and that would be the end of us. No one in the settlement knew that we were here and there was no hope of anyone lowering a rope over the cliff.

By this time we could see that the tide was rising into the rocks. Our only way out of it was if we could climb the high cliff. It really looked impossible, as we could see up above us on the cliff clumps of snow that overhung the top of it. However, we had to decide quickly, for within an hour our lives would be snuffed out by the rising tide!

The weather was quite cold, with showers of snow, and the temperature was 10°F. I decided to attempt climbing the cliff. We each carried a small gaff and after prodding the snow that was banked on the side of the cliff, I found it to be quite hard. It was not ice but hard crusty snow.

I tried to climb and managed to get up 20 feet. The other two fellows did not think much of it; they said if we got up to the top of the cliff, we still would not be able to get in over the brink. This was true and the picture looked grim for our escape. Then Bill, one of my companions, said, "It's the only way to save our lives. We will have to take the chance."

Bill Marlyn was a brave young fellow; this had been proven many times on other adventures I had with him. We were very close companions and had grown up together. The other young fellow was only 11 years of age and looked very frail but proved to be quite tough, in spite of his slight build.

Bill volunteered to take the lead to climb the steep cliff. He said we would put the young fellow, Jimmy, in the middle of the two of us. Thus we tried to scale the 150-foot-high cliff. This cliff is Turks Head, once called Cabot Head, and located between Flat Rock and Torbay on the north side of Torbay.

We made slow progress up the face of the cliff. This was done by drilling holes in the hard snow, making places for our feet. Bill had the hardest job, for he was in the lead and made most of the holes. We finally climbed to a height of 50 feet, and it was the first time I really looked down. I felt giddy and for a few minutes I thought I was going to let go and end it all. There wasn't much to hold on to—only the holes in the hard snow. Then I heard Bill's voice warning us not to look down.

Turks Head, north side of Torbay, first called Cabot Head, where Jack and his two companions scaled the cliff from the ice floe.

Bill kept making progress up the cliff, and we went on. At last Bill reached the top of the cliff face. Now he was up to where this great shelf of snow was hanging over the top of the cliff. He warned Jim and me to hold on as firmly as we could, as he was going to try and break off the hard snow. This was done by prodding it with his gaff and knocking down big chunks of frozen snow.

There were times the chunks fell on our boots and we had difficulty in holding on, but Bill finally succeeded in making a way for his body to crawl over the edge of the cliff. For a few minutes there was no sign of him; then he came to the edge of the cliff and hollered down to us to keep coming up. He also passed down a bit of his hauling rope for us to catch in case we weren't able to make it.

My greatest fear was for Jim, who was next to try to climb over the brink. But without any hesitation the brave little fellow climbed up and without any difficulty went over the top to safety. I had the hardest time of all, for by the time I went to climb over, a lot of the snow that had given footing was broken away. When I finally reached the top, it was because Bill grabbed me in time and kept me from tumbling down. Yes, but for Bill Marlyn, I would not be writing this story!

When all three of us stood on top of the cliff, we found a northwest wind blowing and we had to crawl on our hands and knees to keep from blowing over the cliff again, but, thank God, our lives were saved.

When I was nine, my mother, who had been in poor health for over a year, died, leaving three of us children: Richard, age seven, and sister, Mary, age two. This was a very sad blow to my father and all of us. Just before she died, she made a strange remark. She asked my uncle to drive her to St. John's. Since she was very weak, my uncle thought it very funny she would want to go shopping! He had to help her from the carriage and lead her into the clothing store on Water Street. When she arrived at the counter, the salesman waited on her, and she said to him, "I want to buy two little suits of black clothes and the trimmings that go with them. These are for two little boys, ages seven and nine, to wear to my funeral, for I want them to walk next to my casket."

The salesman she had spoken to was so upset by her request he went inside and sent another salesman to look after her. She died within a month, leaving us all alone to try and manage the best we could. My father did the best he could for us and kept the home going.

At this time we were living down by the Torbay waterfront in the nice home my father had built a few years before my mother died. In the meadow before our front door was a lilac tree. It bloomed every year with loads of lilacs and right there in the shade of the lilac tree my mother used to sit and knit and sew. This was her favourite spot, looking out on the blue waters of Torbay. She died in September, when the lilacs had all faded, and the lilac tree never bloomed again. It looked as if it had died with her.

I learned navigation and received a fair education at Holy Trinity School. Today there is a cemetery where the old schoolhouse stood. They tore down the schoolhouse but they did not tear down the memories of my boyhood days. When I was going to school, it was a boys' school, but not far away was a convent and that's where all the girls attended school, with nuns for teachers.

After school, along Torbay Road, all kinds of fun were carried on among the boys and girls. This is where I first met Kay Dawson, who seemed to be more understanding than the other girls I knew. I started walking her home from school and once in a while we had a date; then I found I was growing very fond of her. Though her name was really Catherine, I called her Kay for short. As the days went by, I found out that she liked me also, and we became childhood sweethearts. She had wavy golden hair with blue eyes and her cheeks were red like roses. There were many fellows after Kay, but they seemed to be very unsuccessful. Our companionship lasted for five years! At this time I left Newfoundland to go to the States, as to go to sea was always in my dreams from childhood. If I really knew what lay ahead of me in my thoughts of high adventure, I would have stayed at home with my flakes and stages in Newfoundland.

CHAPTER 2

The first settler came to Torbay in 1524. This occurred in Torbay Harbour when the vessels from different countries were beginning to come out in the summer and fish, and then go back to their home ports for the winter. Torbay Harbour and the bay constituted quite a wide stretch of water. The vessels at this time were all sailing ships and could manoeuvre better in this wide bay than they could in St. John's. The fishing banks located a few miles off the land were teeming with codfish, and it wasn't long before fishing rooms were located all along the waterfront in Torbay Harbour, where makeshift fishing stages were constructed of rough timbers cut along the shores and rivers of Torbay. Flakes were made up to dry the fish, which would then be packed on board vessels.

It was late in October in 1524 that one of the fishing boats was getting ready to go back to Europe. A fight took place between two of the crew. One was an Irish fellow named Dan McCarthy; the other man's name is not known to me. However, McCarthy hit the other man so hard he knocked him cold on the deck. To the surrounding onlookers, it looked as if the man was dead. For McCarthy's part, it could be the hangman's noose (or the whipping post, which was used at this time). McCarthy took no chances but jumped over the rail and swam for the shore. Quite an effort was made to chase him with boats, but it was a failure. McCarthy just disappeared in the woods and was seen no more by his shipmates.

When all the vessels had left for their homeland, McCarthy found himself stranded on the shores of Newfoundland, to be the first settler in

Torbay. At this time there were quite a few Beothuk Indians along the river that flowed out in the ocean of the west end of Torbay, known today as the Big Beach. To the west of this Big Beach were the waterfalls. The river was known as the Indian River, but today the name has been changed and it is called the Main River.

McCarthy managed to live through his first winter in Torbay. As was a cooper by trade, he put in most of his time making hoops and barrels. He finally made his way to the harbour of St. John's along the seashore that is known today as Marine Drive. There was no trail of any kind to St. John's.

The Beothuks got their livelihood from the sea and the rivers, which were abundant with trout. They went as far up the river as One Island Pond and to the head of what is known as Great Pond on the Bauline Line. From the river there was a trail that ran northwest across to the other side of Conception Bay; to this day, the trail is called the Old Indian Trail. The purpose of these trails used by the Indians was to get seals in Conception Bay, which was a better place for seals than the east coast of Torbay.

The next year when the vessels came out from England and Portugal to start fishing again, McCarthy found out that the man he was supposed to have killed was not dead at all and had come back fishing again. McCarthy built the first log cabin on what is known as Whitty's Hill near Cabot Rock. He lived here himself for two years; then he met an Irish girl who had come out from Ireland to work at the fish, and he married her. Two years after, she went back to Ireland, and when she came back again, she brought with her a sprig from an apple tree. It was growing in a tub and she planted the tree and tub on the hill near the log cabin on the north side of Torbay Harbour. For many years this tree gave out a lot of apples and it is still standing, but it is weathered and silvered. It's a funny thing that no one ever cut it down through all the years, and it still stands as a symbol to our first settlers in Torbay.

Back in 1908 St. John's Harbour was quite a sight with its sailing ships as you walked along the waterfront. The vessels and schooners were so numerous the harbour took on the appearance of a timber forest.

There were schooners from all parts of the bay, for all the trading was done by water. Some produce was carried by the train, which was our famous narrow-gauge track, and the train itself in later years was called the Newfie Bullet. The streets of St. John's were lined with horse carts. Old Water Street had cobblestones, and when the rough wheels with their iron bands went up and down the street, the noise was like thunder.

Many small horse teams came out from the small settlements like Outer Cove, Torbay, Middle Cove, Bauline, and Topsail, when their owners wanted to sell their produce and to shop. The place known today as the War Memorial was called King's Beach and this was an ideal place for tying up and feeding their horses. Goats were a familiar sight in St. John's at this time. They would come up from the sections of Signal Hill and eat the horses' oats which fell out of the feed bags. Many a time a farmer would have oats on his cart in sacks. The quiet goats would climb upon the carts and chew holes in the sacks and eat their fill of oats if not watched. At this time the owners of the ponies, mostly called Torbay nags, chased the goats down the street, cutting the animals with their whips. The horse drivers always had a whip, and when a driver was not whipping something with it, he carried it under his arm, even when he went into a restaurant.

St. John's was made up of many different neighbourhoods, each with its own name: Georgestown, Hoylestown, Monkstown, Rabbit Town, Riverhead, the Battery and the Hole in the Wall, Buckmaster's Field, and the Higher Levels. Most of these names you don't hear mentioned today.

St. John's also at this time had its famous trolley cars. They ran from the railway station up Queens Road along by Rawlins Cross, down Military Road to Duckworth Street, then cut down a short lane known as St. John's Lane to Water Street, and then back to the railway station. This was called "all around the circle," and the people seemed to be well satisfied with this transportation; at least, you would never hear any complaints like we hear today about the buses. The fare was a nickel for the trip.

The old apple tree planted in 1527.

St. John's is the oldest city in North America and has a long history of struggles. As it was the key to Newfoundland since its beginning, the city of St. John's has changed ownership nine times. Many battles were fought in and around St. John's by the English, the French, and others, but in the eighteenth century it was captured for the last time by the British commanded by Captain Cook. Cook landed an army at Torbay and some claim that no fighting was done either at Torbay or around St. John's. This is not true, as the people who lived in Torbay gave an account of the capture of St. John's by the British.

A part of the French army was stationed at Torbay at the time, with guns mounted on the north side of the harbour. One was on Gosse's Hill, another at Treasure Cove Hill, and another on what is called Slow Trees at the entrance to Torbay Harbour that is still called the Battery. I remember them well. There were five guns on this Battery that fired the cannonballs and they were still standing there in the early part of the nineteenth century.

At the time Cook landed on the west beach of Torbay, these guns were in use, but Cook was a very shrewd commander and found out that the guns would not do him much harm if he came up the south side of the harbour. The only gun that could cause him any damage was the one on the west side, called the Battery. (He was out of range of the guns on the north shore.) After some 800 or 1,000 of his men got ashore, Cook was met by the French near the mouth of the river. Some fighting was done all around this section and on the hill leading up to what is Torbay Road, today.

After the fighting was over, one of the officers said to the captain, "Well, you took the hill."

The captain answered, "We took the hill, but it was costly." And now it's called Costly Hill in Torbay.

The soldiers were buried along the bank of the river, but in later years the bodies were moved to the old cemetery on the south side of Torbay. They were buried in unmarked graves. They are the unknown soldiers of Torbay.

The route of the army was along the way that Torbay Road now runs. When they got to Pulpit Rock, the army divided into two groups—one followed the route straight to St. John's, by going south; the other group travelled to the west and then came out in the direction of where the Confederation Building now stands. The two groups merged at Quidi Vidi, where the surrender of St. John's took place. This was the last time it was taken by the British army (Captain Cook's soldiers).

I may add that, where the army divided, a wedding took place. Miss Coady (by all accounts her name was Catherine) was married by one of the captains of the army to a British soldier. It was here on this rock that one of the British officers preached a short sermon to his men, with the young bride and groom in their midst, and the rock got its name—Pulpit Rock.

Newfoundland is noted for ghost stories and buried treasure. In many parts of the island, people have their stories of loot buried by the pirates. Among them was the story of the *Flying Cloud*, Captain Kidd, and many other pirates who sailed the Spanish Main and flew the skull and crossbones.

In the early part of the eighteenth century the people of Torbay were awakened by gunfire and, to their surprise, the *Flying Cloud* was anchored in Torbay Harbour. At this time, there was no information about her being a pirate ship; the crew visited the shores of Torbay, where they enjoyed dancing and were treated well by the people of the settlement. She afterwards became an outstanding pirate ship and had some Newfoundlanders in her crew; but, as the story goes, these Newfoundlanders did not take part in her slave running or piracy on the Spanish Main. It is not known for sure if the crew of the *Flying Cloud* buried any of her stolen treasures in Torbay, but it was after her appearance that stories of buried treasure started circulating through the community.

Treasure Cove on the north side of Torbay is where two treasures are supposed to be buried and became noted for its ghost stories. It started when two fishermen returned late from the fishing grounds one night, their boat loaded with fish. After landing on Sandy Beach at Treasure Cove, a black dog came walking down toward the boat. The fishermen thought it was a village dog, but they were in for a surprise. As the dog approached them, its two eyes had a fiery glare that was very frightening. There was a rattling of chain and behind the dog a man with no head appeared! The two fishermen tried to push the boat from the sand to escape from this dreadful scene, but they had difficulty in moving the boat in the sand because of the weight of the fish. By this time the beach rocks were rattling and the noise was so loud they thought the cliff was tumbling down on top of them. After great difficulty, they managed to get their boat afloat and they rowed away from the dreadful ordeal in Treasure Cove. They spent the remainder of the night anchored in the harbour.

One of them, Henry Fulton, became an invalid. The other man, whose name was Tapper, died a year after, and Treasure Cove became a dreadful place. Nobody would dare venture in the cove after that night.

Jack Dodd standing in the haunted Treasure Cove.

The story goes that, when the treasure was buried, the pirates had a young lad with them, the cabin boy, who was about 15 years old, and the ship's dog, a Newfoundland dog which was very friendly to the boy. The pirate captain asked, "Who will take a mark to where this treasure is buried so that it will be guarded?"

The young lad said, "Sir, I will."

With this, the captain cut off the boy's head, and the dog attacked him. He then cut off the dog's head, and the dog and the boy were buried near the treasure in Treasure Cove. This bears out the story of the big black dog and the man with no head that has been told down through the years.

Shortly after this a Spanish galleon was towed into Torbay Harbour by a pirate ship. She was captured somewhere off the Newfoundland coast and was said to be loaded with gold bullion. The pirates landed in Tapper's Cove (as it is now called, but then it was called Diamond Cove). The gold bricks were buried along the riverbank, and while they were busy bringing them ashore in their longboats, they were attacked by a pirate ship from the sea. The cannonballs flew everywhere. Some of these cannonballs were dug up years after in Torbay. So you can see that this settlement had a blustery history.

The Spanish galleon was scuttled by her captors to keep her from being invaded by pirates. She is supposed to be sunk off a place called Cheer Cove, in Gallows Cove on the north side of Torbay. If she is still there, there is gold bullion lying off the shores of Torbay. Twelve of the pirates were tried and hanged in Gallows Cove and this is how the place got its name. The scaffold where the buccaneers were hanged was still standing in the early part of the nineteenth century; later what was left of it was thrown over the cliff.

There is every indication that some of this very treasure has been found, especially at Treasure Cove, because, after all this had taken place, a strange man appeared in Torbay. I suppose I can refer to him as Peg Leg, as his leg was gone from the hip. He claimed to be the brother of a man in Torbay whose name was George McDonald. He said it was his lost brother who had been gone for years, but I am doubtful, for I really think he was a pirate. He was hard of hearing and I think this was caused by gunfire on the pirate ships (it might have ruptured his eardrums). He never told anything about himself or his travels. He said his name was Joe McDonald, but he was called Peg Leg most of the time. It seems that he had made the leg himself; it was a clumsy job, and he had difficulty walking with it.

Peg Leg set himself up as a shoemaker in a little shack he had built with a deep cellar underneath it. It was a mystery why he had this cellar because he never kept any vegetables in it, and in those days cellars were used for keeping potatoes and turnips from getting frostbitten. He was not a real shoemaker, for the work he did on shoes lacked a tradesman's touch.

I went to visit him many times in his rough surroundings. His utensils consisted of an old iron kettle, an iron pot, and a bakepot. Thus he kept house and lived the life of a hermit, except that he was surrounded by many neighbours in the community. He was a very peculiar man indeed and was considered a mystery by all the people in the settlement.

One night two girls called on him to get some shoes. He was deaf and always left his door unlocked. Since there was no sense in knocking, the girls walked in. He did not notice them when they entered as he was engaged in what he was looking at and his back was turned to them. He was settled at the table and on it a lantern and a kitchen lamp were burning. Spread out on the table was a map. As far as the girls could see, the map was very rough and wrinkled and it looked as if it was a piece of brown canvas with white markings. Very plainly it was the drawing of a sailing ship with what seemed to be the shores of a piece of land. One thing the girls managed to read was the name of the port: "East Bay," meaning Torbay. After seeing the girls, he hurriedly folded the map and put it in his bedroom, which was nearby.

When the girls first told me this story, it occurred to me that Peg Leg either was a pirate or had some connections with pirates in his time!

The map was a mystery for a long time. One night I was returning from Tapper's Cove, where I was engaged in the fishery. It was between midnight and 1 a.m. As I was walking, I heard some noise on the upper side of the road where there was a garden and a horse pond. I stopped and listened for a while to detect what was making the sounds. When I discovered it was someone digging in the garden, I crawled up on my hands and knees to find out what it was all about. I then made out the form of a man digging in the garden. He had quite a hole dug with clay thrown up on the side. To my surprise it was Peg Leg Joe. But what surprised me more was why he was digging at this late hour and in someone else's garden. Then I remembered the map! He was digging for one of the buried treasures!

I did not make any disturbance to let him know I was spying on him, because, if he knew, he might have killed me with his pickaxe. So I returned to the road as silently as I could and made my way home from Treasure Cove. I did not sleep much that night, with the thoughts of the map in my mind and then seeing the old man digging in the garden. It seemed to make sense that this man was on the trail of the buried treasure. I could not tell the man who owned the garden about it, for he would make trouble for Peg Leg Joe and bring me into it. There was only one way out: to keep it to myself.

The next morning I went back to where I had seen him digging in the garden and the place was so well levelled off and graded you could hardly tell that anyone had been working there. There were no vegetables in this garden as it was just before planting time, so nobody noticed that the soil in the garden on the west side of Treasure Cove had ever been disturbed.

I visited the old shoemaker's shop on at least two occasions after and somehow he seemed to be more in good spirits than at any time I had seen him before. After this he seemed to be drinking more and at least once or twice I saw him drunk; Peg Leg really liked his rum and drank Demerara rum, which was his favourite.

One night my father sent me to get a pair of leather boots that Peg

Leg was mending. It was 11:30 p.m. when I arrived at the shoemaker's shop. A dim light was burning in the small window which was in his kitchen. I tried the door, which was unlocked, and I walked in. Peg Leg was not sitting in the chair (which he used while mending shoes). I noticed his room door was open and he was sitting on the side of his bed. His back was toward me and he never noticed me looking on.

There was a battered chest by the bed and also a worn piece of canvas that looked like a sea bag. The hinges on the old chest were rusted and seemed to be in bad shape. There was a pile of gold on one part of the bed which I would say amounted to thousands of dollars. Then in another pile was silver and in another pile there were more pieces of money which I couldn't recognize. There were rolls of paper laid on the foot of the bed. This paper money—I couldn't tell what currency it was— seemed to have been water-soaked and then dried out. It was spooky looking, but it was the most money I had ever seen in my life.

He was so busy counting the money and throwing it in different places that he never turned around to notice me. Then fear came over me. If he saw me spying on him, God knows what he would do to me! I stole out of the house. I had to get the boots for my father, so I decided to go out on the road and wait for an hour. I then went back and knocked at the door of the people who lived nearby and got the lady (out of bed) to go back to Peg Leg's with me.

When we arrived there, all the lights were out, but she had a way of getting his attention although he could hear no sounds of any kind. She got a rock and pounded on the side of the shack. By pounding on the side of his shack, and thus shaking the shack, she got Peg Leg out to the door. He wasn't very pleased, but he finally gave me my father's boots and I paid him his money.

Peg Leg died two years after that and at the time of his death I was surprised when his friends told me he never had one nickel to bury him. So the mystery of the treasure I had seen on the bed goes unsolved. I think he buried the treasure again, but where, no one knows.

Some years after I searched Treasure Cove with a Geiger counter and, after having no success, I tried an old house that was still standing on the banks near the ocean.

This house had been built in the seventeenth century and had quite a history of its own. On entering through the gateposts the Geiger counter registered five on its meter—this could indicate gold or silver or some other precious metal. It seemed to be only in one place, so I drew a circle all around the counter. This circle measured about 9 feet across and it was just inside of this circle that the counter would work, indicating that some mineral lay underneath the ground.

As it was on private property, I could not dig; I asked the owner's permission, but I was refused.

If treasure is buried, it is still to be proven, and the house is now in ruins. The people moved away from there some years ago and the place was abandoned. It was once a beautiful home, set in a grove of willow, lilac, and gooseberry trees.

The surrounding waterfront was most beautiful. Many people were engaged in the fishery. Fishing boats were to be seen coming in and out of the bay. Smoke came from the cook shacks, and both men and women were working at the fishing industry. But all of this changed when Newfoundland joined Confederation and our new provincial government took the reins to guide the province. The cry of "burn your boats" could be heard all over the island. "Don't stay in them like your fathers did." But this propaganda never did materialize in Newfoundland. The poor fishermen, I think, believed this propaganda, and it was a familiar sight to see the fishing boats going up in smoke. This was not done by the fishermen themselves but by the young people, and the Torbay fishing community became a ghost fishing village.

The fishermen were to learn later that the prosperity promised them by the Newfoundland government never did happen and they had to return to the fishery with no fishing boats left to go fishing in. Then there came the struggle to get boats and start all over again and try to build up the shore fishery while the government gave them no help. Both our federal and Newfoundland governments are very backward in building up our shore fishery. All they are doing is building draggers and trawlers, putting them in the bays of Newfoundland, and destroying the young fish stocks and the fishermen's nets and traps. This kind of a plan by the government is the ruination of the shore fishery.

If the government of Canada would abandon all stern trawlers, side trawlers, and draggers of all sizes, foreign and Canadian, including Newfoundland, and put them out a distance of 50 miles away from the bays of especially the east coast of Newfoundland, this limit would be the greatest step in the right direction to preserve our fish stocks and save our shore fishery. If this is not done, we will find our fishery in the same predicament as that in the USA—no fish.

The first place of worship where Mass and prayer were performed was on the north side of Torbay Harbour. It was a long house with a "soddy" roof built of logs and all its seams stuffed with moss. This was in the sixteenth century, and when vessels were anchored in the harbour, the crews went to church there. The people were Irish, Scottish, and English. This place was used for years, well up in the seventeenth century.

In 1833 the first church was built on the south side of the harbour. This church lasted for quite a few years before it was torn down and replaced by a stone chapel. The stone chapel was built in 1859 and was four stories high with a shingled roof. There was a belfry nearby with a bell that could be heard for a distance of 6 miles. For some reason this bell was changed and replaced by the bell that stands today near the new church, about 3 miles from the stone chapel. The convent built in the latter part of the nineteenth century is midway between the old stone chapel and the new wooden frame church that now stands overlooking the ocean on the south side of the harbour.

Getting back to the stone chapel that had served the people for many years, it was built by the Reverend Father Troy. Then as the years went by, the roof decayed and it was too dangerous to have Mass there any longer. After the new church was erected in the early part of the twentieth century, the old church was abandoned and then the roof caved in and fell down. I described this in the song I wrote called "The Valleys of Torbay":

There is an old stone chapel standing on the wall,
Its roof has gone to pieces and now begun to fall,
Inside of this stone chapel on a fine summer day,
I received Holy Baptism in the valleys of Torbay!

Since this song was written, the church has fallen and its stones are piled around the foundation. The stone is not native to Newfoundland; it was brought from a foreign country. When Reverend Father Troy died, he was buried underneath the stone chapel, where his remains lay for over 50 years. When the new chapel was built, and consecrated, the remains of Father Troy were removed and buried underneath the new chapel.

It is said that Reverend Troy, after 50 years buried, had not decayed, and he was placed on display in the aisle of the new church for people. I did not see him myself, but I was in a conversation with a friend who had gone to see him and, as he said, the priest looked the same as when he was alive!

A plaque was erected by the parishioners of Torbay to the memory of their late beloved pastor, who was for 30 years their spiritual guide:

By his many virtues he endeared himself to all who knew him and had
the privilege of his wise counsel. In the face of affliction he was ever a
steadfast friend. In times of trouble he was always an unerring guide,
to the noblest characteristics of the Christian priesthood. He had many
endearing social qualities and this attracted the veneration and es-
teem of his devoted flock. He was called to the reward of his labours on
April 2, 1972, in the 75th year of his age and the 45th of his ministry.
He was born in the year 1797 and died in 1872.

In the Torbay area we have Outer Cove, Middle Cove, Newton, Bullockstown, Indian Meal Line, and Bauline Line. All these places are known as Torbay. Torbay Harbour, which takes in from the north and south sides of the harbour to the Bauline Line and Gallows Cove, is known as Torbay proper.

Holy Trinity Catholic Church, Torbay, 1919,
consecrated by Archbishop Roche.

The Church of England was built near the big beach on the west end of the harbour. It was a small wooden structure. The church was built in the early part of the eighteenth century and here the Church of England people worshipped for over a hundred years. It was finally torn down and a new church built upon the hill in 1924. The new church now standing on the hill is one of the most beautiful churches in Newfoundland. When the chimes ring out it makes one feel joyous and awakens bygone memories.

St. Nicholas Anglican Church, Torbay, built and consecrated in 1924.

Outer Cove, known as Torbay South, is a fishing community and right here we had the famous crew who rowed the "9.13." This is a standing record time rowed on Quidi Vidi Lake in St. John's East in 1901. There were four boats taking part in this famous race. Two crews were from Torbay Harbour, which is known as Torbay North. One of the crews held the championship at this time and in the morning in the fishermen's race beat Outer Cove and retained the championship. In the afternoon of the same day in the championship race, they were defeated by the Outer Cove crew. This was a stunning upset for the Torbay champions and also to the thousands of racing fans who lined the banks of Quidi Vidi Lake on this fine sunny day.

I have investigated this story and talked to some 200 eyewitnesses who watched the race from the west bank of the lake. The race was what they called "neck and neck" to the finish line. As some of them told me, you could not detect any difference in the boats—it was so close. One man maintained it was a dead heat to win and would need a camera to distinguish the difference, if any. In other words, it was a photo finish. After about 30 minutes, the judges finally decided in favour of the Outer Cove crew and the record of "9.13" was established for the Regatta.

The Regatta is the biggest sporting day in Newfoundland. There are conflicting stories down through Newfoundland history as to when the racing on Quidi Vidi Lake first began, but according to my investigations it started in the seventeenth century. At this time many ships from foreign countries were trading and visiting Newfoundland, and two crews challenged one another to have a race. The race between English and Irish, using lifeboats, was held in Torbay Harbour.

The crew from the English ship won the race. The trophy for the champions was a bottle of rum for each of the four men in a crew, with the coxswain who steered the boat making five in all. This race did not go off without trouble and a fight took place between the English and Irish. They challenged each other for a return race. The next year it was blowing too hard in Torbay Harbour, so the two lifeboats were taken to Quidi Vidi Lake.

The day, date, and year are not known, but there is no doubt that the first race on the lake was between an English and an Irish crew. This time the Irish beat the English and became the first champions of the Regatta on Quidi Vidi Lake. It is famous today for its shell racing, with two outstanding fast records: one by the Outer Cove crew, 9.13 and four-tenths, and one by a Torbay Harbour crew, 9.29.

St. John's, Newfoundland, is famous for its seal hunting. Down through our history we had good fleets of sealing ships. We could call this "back in the good old days," when our Newfoundland seal hunters really went down to the sea in ships. There were the Bowrings, Baine Johnstons (then called Grieves), Harveys, Bairds, Jobs, and other merchants doing business along Water Street in St. John's and who were owners and agents for both sailing ships and steamships. The merchants were the friends of the fishermen of Newfoundland, although, at the time, they were sometimes criticized and classed as thieves. But this is not true.

Take cod fishing: This shore fishery was made up of trap men trawling and handlining. There were no draggers or beam trawlers in the early part of the Newfoundland fishery, but in later years beam trawlers, draggers, and gill netters were introduced into the fishery and today are the cause of destruction to fishing gear and of our stocks of all species of fish. The shore fishermen today are hampered by this type of fishing.

Our salmon fishery is also hampered by the new regulations enforced by the authorities. May 15 is not the right date for setting salmon nets. The poor fisherman after a long hungry winter is not allowed to set his nets until May 15. In years gone by when the fishermen had the freedom of the seas, there were no dates for setting nets and salmon were caught around April 12. The fisherman sometimes had his money made before May 15. Now the fisherman has a noose around his neck and it is getting tighter all the time. The blame for all this is our government rule-makers, who will automatically destroy our Newfoundland fishing industry. Getting back to the merchants, in days gone by they were good to the fisherman. The fisherman could go out to the merchant in the early spring and get his supply of food and fishing gear—all on credit.

The fisherman and his family did not have anything to worry about, and he had a market for his fish. The merchant bought all the fish he could get from around the island of Newfoundland. When the bills were paid to the merchant, he took very little interest for his money. Therefore, as I stated before, I think the merchants of Newfoundland were the great friends of the fisherman!

Every spring berths were given to go to the ice to hunt the whitecoats and most everyone who wanted to take part could sail in a sealing ship. But today all this is gone. Our Newfoundland merchants were by all accounts forced out of the cod and seal fishery, and Water Street has already taken on a ghost town look with only one or two little sealing ships whose owners can't make up their minds if they will send them to the seal fishery or not. We know that the actions now going on by the Humane Societies are hampering the seal fishery and there is always someone coming into the picture to do more bad than good for the seal fishery of Newfoundland. If these rules are kept, the sealing and cod fishing that were once so famous in our Newfoundland history will disappear.

CHAPTER 3

In 1922 I made my first trip to the seal fishery. This was on the SS *Diana*, better known in those days as the *Hector*. About eight ships took part in this seal hunt. We sailed out from St. John's on March 10. It was an impressive sight, one ship after the other going through the Narrows with clouds of black coal smoke going in over the north side of St. John's Harbour. Although it was early in the morning, there were crowds of people at the Battery waving to the ships as they steamed out the Narrows.

Diana *at the seal fishery. Later lost in March 1922.*

When the *Diana* got about 1 mile off St. John's, the crew discovered five stowaways on board. The captain decided to turn the ship around and have the stowaways landed, but we did not go into St. John's—they were taken off by a small tugboat and returned to port. These stowaways were not a bit pleased and shouted all kinds of abuse at us. But the ship once more was on her way, though about two hours had been lost. These two hours put us back quite a lot, and when we finally got going, the other ships were out of sight steaming toward Cape St. Francis.

By this time the ice jam that was close to the shore kept pressing on us and the *Diana* could only get down as far as Cape St. Francis. She had to change course, head out east, and try to work her way through the heavy ice. The captain was disappointed and kept saying we would lose the opportunity of getting into the seals off the Funks. They all were wrong, for in this particular case of seal hunting our setback was to prove profitable; at least, it put us in a position to strike the seals.

All afternoon and all night the *Diana* kept making slow progress through the heavy ice, the captain trying to work her to the north. Our position at this time was off Cape St. Francis somewhere east-northeast in a heavy jam of ice. The captain was walking the bridge and he looked like he could chew nails and spit rust, he was so mad. Yes, the captain of the *Diana* thought he had made a mistake and the five little stowaways that we had to land were the cause of it.

On March 12, while steaming through the heavy ice, two polar bears were sighted and not far from them two white foxes.

As the polar bears were a long distance from the ship, there was no way of telling what they were eating, but the captain claimed they were eating fish that were brought up on the ice by the seals. No one seemed to pay much attention to his statement, but about five hours after he was proved right when the man in the crow's nest shouted down to the deck that there were seals ahead. This brought the captain and the mate out on the bridge. They trained their spyglasses in the direction of where the man in the crow's nest had pointed—about five points on the starboard bow.

It wasn't long before that the whitecoats could be seen from the deck, on the port and starboard sides. This was about 4 p.m., March 13, and by 10 p.m. the *Diana* was in a patch of seals. The cries of the seals in the darkness indicated that there were thousands of them around the ship.

We weren't allowed to kill seals until March 15 but the men used to go over the side and bring whitecoats on board in their arms. There were times when there was no room for walking on the deck, there were so many whitecoats. Then, the captain gave them orders to put them over the side and would not allow any of the whitecoats to be killed. We had to wait until 4 a.m. on March 15.

This was my first trip to the seal fishery and also my first trip on a ship. In other words, my first ship! But little did I dream what lay ahead of all of us on the good ship *Diana*. If one could look into the future and see what is ahead, I think it would be very discouraging. However, for the present, everything was the beginning of a new adventure. The ship's whistle blew about 4 a.m. This was the signal to go over the side. Men were rushing with their gaffs, hauling ropes, and confusion was all around as they hit the ice and started to kill the young seals. We killed seals all day. Sometimes we would sculp some but most of the time was spent at the killing. The killing was done by giving the whitecoat a crack on the nose with the hook end of the gaff.

Sometimes an experienced seal hunter killed a whitecoat by hitting him with the heel of his boot. I don't remember seeing any of these seals come back to life. They just lay there dead until they were sculped.

Now this is what is meant by sculping a seal. The seal hunter has a very sharp knife which he carries in a shield. This shield is made of leather—a casing for the knife. It is carried on a belt around the seal hunter's waist. Also attached to the same belt is a piece of steel. This is for sharpening the knife. The knife must have a razor-like edge to cut through the very thick fur.

In order to sculp the whitecoat, the knife is drawn from its head to his hind part near the tail. The whitecoat is ripped open all along the belly part. The knife then cuts the flipper string on both left and right sides. This is done to render the flippers useless, and the inexperienced seal hunter is warned to be sure and do this. If the seal came back to life, it could scratch the seal hunter's face or hands with its sharp claw nails.

In this operation I myself opened 180 seals but I never saw one come back to life. We killed seals until 4 p.m. March 15. Then the ship blew her whistle to stop killing, as a load of seals were already on the ice for the *Diana*. They afterwards said we killed 38,000 whitecoats.

The work then began, taking the pelts off them, which means sculping. It was a true slaughter when you looked at it. No adult seals were killed but the way the mother seals acted was a heart-rending sight to see. The mother seal would come back to where she had left her young one to find its carcass lying near the hole. She would turn, move and go around in circles and sometimes put her nose to the carcass as if she was crying in her deep sorrow. A similar performance was carried out by the father seal, which is referred to as a harp seal.

Each seal has a hole in the ice, which is called the bobbin hole by seal hunters. It is kept open by the adult seal coming up and down from the water to the top of the ice. It makes no difference how cold it is, this hole is always kept open. At the side of this bobbin hole is where the mother seal leaves her young one. She nurses it early in the morning, then goes away to search for food and returns in the evening, as the young seal is nursed twice a day.

It is very dangerous working near the bobbin hole—the inexperienced seal hunter is instructed by the master watch never to turn his back to the opening, for, if the mother seal comes up behind the man, she could tear him to pieces. So in sculping the young seal, the hunter must always face the opening in the ice.

Accidents have happened to seal hunters who failed to follow the rules. On one occasion a man was working with his back to the bobbin hole. The mother seal came up, grabbing the man and sinking her teeth deep into his back. The poor man got an awful tearing up, which caused his death. Many accidents happened down through the years in our Newfoundland seal fishery, but most of them were just forgotten and never appeared in the press.

Everything seemed to be going well on our seal hunt at this time.

Then on March 16, while we were working some 5 miles from the ship, 20 men were caught out on the ice. I was one of them. However, as it was my first experience, I did not mind very much and didn't realize how serious this could prove. It happened when a great body of water opened between the men and the ship, and we could not travel back to the *Diana*, which was jammed in the ice. As darkness came on, showers of snow were falling with the temperature -10°F.

Lucky for us, we had our master watch with us, who was an experienced man by the name of Leo Butt. He kept the men running around the pan of ice to keep warm. We could not start a fire; we made many attempts to do so but failed to get it going. It looked very much like we were all going to die on the ice that night, but about 1 a.m. our hopes were kindled by seeing a light. It proved to be a ship steaming down the body of open water. Everyone started to holler out to get the ship's attention.

Sometimes when a squall of snow would come the ship's lights would be lost from view, but then at last she came in the Narrows. The captain of the ship hollered out and asked who we were and what ship we belonged to. We told him the *Diana*, and he informed us the *Diana* was jammed in the ice about 8 miles away. This was the SS *Thetis*, commanded by Captain William Winsor. The *Thetis* was owned by Job Brothers in St. John's and was one of the sealing ships taking part in the seal hunt of 1922.

We were taken on board and treated well by the captain and the crew. After we were settled, the captain came down in the forecastle and ordered a full mug of Demerara rum for each man in the *Diana*'s crew. Then about 6 a.m. we were put on the ice to walk to the *Diana* 8 miles away. The morning was frosty but clear and the master watch had the course set to the ship.

We reached our ship by 4 p.m. By this time the *Diana* had just broken loose from the ice jam and was again picking up her seals. She had 8,500 young harps on board; she had 38,000 killed altogether—it was a full load for her. This was March 16, and the talk of all the men was that we would be ready for home by March 19, with probably one of the quickest trips ever made. But we were all in for a surprise, which proves it is not a good policy to plan ahead.

The patch of seals we were in was north of the main patch. While we were killing seals, the *Diana*'s captain had sent out a search party, which travelled 7 miles to the main patch, and they brought back the news of their discovery. They estimated the main patch to be 40 miles long and 20 miles wide, with approximately 2 million seals on it. This was big news to the captain of the *Diana*, who wasn't satisfied with being in a small patch and by all accounts tried to get his ship to the main patch of seals. If he intended to take on board the seals he killed, we don't know, but, from the start of the news, he kept working the *Diana* in the direction of the main patch. The heaviest ice he would have to go through was about 1 mile; this he kept butting at all the late afternoon and did not seem to be picking up the seals that he could easily have taken on board—the ones already killed and sculped.

We were butting at the barrier of ice late up in the night, with men out ahead of the ship on the hauling line blasting the ice with cans of powder, while the ship kept going ahead and astern butting at the ice barrier. While these men were engaged in hauling on the line, they kept singing shanty songs like "Sally Brown," "Come Down, I Tell You," "Hoe a Hoe," "Roll and Go, Roll and Go When She Rolled Me Over," "Spent My Money on You, Sally Brown," and "Jolly Poker."

The singing and hauling went on until 11 p.m., March 16, at which time the men were called on board, but the ship kept butting the ice barrier. About 11:30 p.m., while the ship was going astern, her propeller hit a lump of ice with such an impact it shook the ship from stem to stern. She lay still while an examination was made by her engineers. They reported to the captain that the ship's main shaft was broken. This meant that the *Diana* was all through with either getting to the main patch or picking up the seals her crew had already killed.

There was disappointment among all the crew members, for they all knew that the expected quick trip was over and the ship was adrift in the great ice floe on the North Atlantic. The jam of ice we were in proved to be what they called a rafter, which is very dangerous for a ship to get caught in. There were times in the morning of March 17, St. Patrick's Day, when we thought the ship's sides would come together from the pressure of the ice.

Pans of ice started coming over the rail and as fast as the men would cut the ice in pieces and throw it overboard, it would come back again. Then a very strange thing happened. The ice nipped the ship as though she was a matchbox, forcing her right up out of the water and up on top of the ice, high and dry, as though she was some little toy ship.

Men began scrambling over the side and away from the ship, some dragging their belongings with them. They kept going over the side until almost all the crew were off the ship, but Captain Parsons was still clinging to the bridge and telling the men there was no danger.

The ship lay on the ice on her side. Her propeller was in view and it did not seem that there was anything the matter with it. However, the main shaft was broken inside the stuffing box (which is called the shaft casing). The ship lay on her side for about two hours and then she started to settle back in the water. We slid into the water as if an unseen hand was settling her back and became upright again.

The crew went back on board to face the misery and dangers of the days ahead. The captain, who had clung to the bridge even when the ship lay on the ice on her side, was furious with the stowaways, whom he blamed for causing so much bad luck at the start of the voyage. Now to make things worse, three more stowaways were discovered and brought before the captain—two of them were 14 and 15 in age, but outstanding was one little fellow aged 10!

After the captain asked them why they had stowed away, they gave a good explanation. They wanted to get to the ice in the hopes they would be signed on when discovered. They were put to work with the rest of the crew, but the captain seemed to be more interested in the little fellow, who was a tough customer. He wore a pair of long leather boots about four sizes too big for him. His little coat was torn in many places and the little pair of coveralls he wore had several patches. He had a red stocking cap on his head with a white tassel on the top. His face was so dirty it looked as if it hadn't been washed for weeks. To crown it all, he was chewing tobacco like a goat.

When the captain scolded him for running away from school, he said, "I don't see any use in going to school. It seems like a lot of lost time. I wanted to go to sea. That's why when I got the opportunity I stowed away on this ship."

The captain then asked him, "Don't you know I could put you in irons for stowing away?"

His answer was, "Well, sir, you are the captain and what you say is OK with me. If you put me in irons, it will still be better than going to school."

The captain questioned, "What do you have in your mouth?"

The little stowaway replied, "It's a chew of tobacco."

"You had better get that chew out of your mouth," the captain ordered, "and don't let me catch you chewing tobacco again."

"Well, captain, I can't promise you, as I got to have my chew of tobacco." The captain asked him his name, and he said, "William Doyle, but, captain, you can call me Bill if you wish. It's OK with me."

The captain looked at the master watch, who was standing beside him on the bridge, and a big smile came on the captain's face. He then spoke to the little stowaway again: "Now, Bill, you will be put to work helping the after-cooks. I hope you are good at peeling potatoes."

The stowaway asked, "Captain, will I still have to go in irons?"

So Bill, the stowaway, was put to work with the after-cooks.

The seriousness of our situation was uppermost in our minds. We were back in the water with our ship helpless and at the mercy of the waves. We were in the heavy ice and drifting to the south. The first night we were broken down, a storm came. The wind was from the northeast about 60 miles an hour and bringing a blinding snowstorm. It was so bad on the deck of the ship that many men were kept busy shovelling snow, and at times you could not see the man in front of you. The word was going around among the crew to send out an SOS. Some said that an SOS was sent out, but no true statement was received by us that a message for help had been sent from the *Diana*. The storm lasted all night, up to noon the next day, March 19.

When the storm was over, the ship had drifted into a city of icebergs. Towers of ice could be seen all around us. We counted 110 icebergs in all. This was very dangerous because if the ship came in contact with an iceberg, it would tumble down on her, thus crushing her to pieces. The captain now gave orders to hoist the canvas. Every bit of sail we could get on her was hoisted aloft. As the *Diana* was both sail and steam, she had three masts square-rigged. On the foremast she had one yardarm and on the mizzen-mast one yardarm; on the main she carried a riding sail; and she also had two top sails, one on the foremast and one on the main mast. The yards were all equipped with canvas, and once again the *Diana* was turned into a sailing ship!

With the help of the sails we would be able to manoeuvre her clear of the icebergs, providing the wind lasted to fill the sails. But efforts to keep clear of one iceberg failed, and the ship drifted down on top of it. This berg was about three stories high over the ship with a big arm of ice protruding from the iceberg. This big arm of ice went between the ship's mizzen and foremast, and confusion was caused among the crew. Men were running for axes to chop the ice, but the captain hollered down a stern command from the bridge not to touch the ice with axes. He threatened to shoot the first man who chopped at the iceberg. The reason: if any chopping was done, the iceberg could founder and crush the ship to pieces. His command was obeyed!

The ship was turned around by the iceberg three times and everyone was frightened to death, expecting any minute that the iceberg would founder and it would be the end of us all. But luck was with us and the ship seemed to be going clear of the hook of ice. She was almost free except that one of the lumps of ice on the arm was holding her in the lower yardarm on the foremast. It looked to me that if someone went up and cut the ropes that seemed to be wrapped around the ice, the ship would go free. I climbed up the rigging, out over the yardarm, and with my sealing knife I cut the two lines free of ice.

After the second line was cut, a crash was heard and the yardarm broke underneath my feet. The ship rolled to the starboard and went clear of the iceberg. I had a very narrow escape with my life.

It was only by chance I grabbed a rope and swung back onto the unbroken piece of what was left of the yardarm. As I scrambled down to the deck, thinking I was a hero, I got a bawling out from the captain. He claimed I should never have gone up there without his orders, but my fellow shipmates felt differently about it. They all complimented me on risking my life and freeing the ship from the iceberg.

We had many close encounters with icebergs in the days that followed and a lot of misery was suffered by all of our crew. Then, on our fourth day adrift we sighted the *Thetis*. We sent some men aboard and found out that the *Thetis* had her bow broken in. Hopes were with our men, who were thinking that Captain Winsor of the *Thetis* would take the *Diana*'s crew off or try to tow her into port. But no efforts were made to do anything for us. Then on March 20 we lost sight of the *Thetis*. She had just disappeared from view and again our hopes had fallen.

Every morning someone would be sent from the bridge to read a message to us saying that some ship was coming out from St. John's to tow us in. Some believed this, but the experienced seal hunters among us said this would be impossible because there was no ship in St. John's powerful enough to tow the *Diana* from the jam of ice that now surrounded her. There was a great deal of discouragement among our crew, and they decided it was time to send out an SOS.

The ship was leaking badly and only could be kept afloat by her steam pumps. Our coal was running low, for in taking on board 8,500 seals, we had thrown a lot of our coal away on the ice to make room for the seals. We had also thrown away about 20 barrels of beef and pork and 20 bags of hard tack. All this was done to make room for storing the seals on board, but, now, adrift in a helpless ship, we began to feel that we should have kept the coal and food that had been thrown away.

There were times when some of the men who had families at home began to cry and among the 130 men there was a lot of discouragement. As I was a young fellow, I did not understand what dangers were in store, but the experienced seal hunters knew what could happen and were leaving no stone unturned to try to get out of the dangerous predicament we were in. With so much discontent it looked as if mutiny could come at any time.

One afternoon our first master watch came down among the crew and said, "Men, I have something to tell you." As he was a very close friend of the captain, we gathered around him, expecting he had some good news for us. But we were all in for a big surprise. "Men," he told us, "all those messages which have been read to you regarding ships coming to rescue us are untrue. We never received any messages from anywhere. It is time for us to stand up and demand an SOS be sent out as we stand in danger of this helpless ship going down any time. So it is up to you now to demand that the captain send out an SOS."

Well, that started it. So many men were picked out to go to the Marconi room and take it over. Among the crew was a Marconi man. He was put in with the two wireless operators and the demanded SOS was sent out. To back this up, all the crew took part in a march aft on the cabin. The captain was against sending out the SOS, but under the circumstances he had no power to stop it. Some of the men were so much enraged over the false messages which they blamed the captain for sending to them they tried to get down in the cabin where the captain was. However, they were told by the captain that he would take drastic actions against them if they should venture into the cabin.

One hundred and twenty men took part in this mutiny, for I will call it a mutiny, on the *Diana* to send out the SOS. Guards were stationed at the Marconi room and cabin. Men were stationed with sealing guns at these places; some had drawn hunting knives just to make sure that their demands weren't interrupted by the captain or any of his men in the cabin.

It took some 24 hours after the mutiny started and the SOS was sent out before we got an answer. At last the Marconi man received a message from the *Ranger*. She was the first ship to pick up our signal. She was also disabled, with a broken propeller, but she sent cheerful news—she had relayed our message to the SS *Sagona* and the *Sagona* was on her way to us.

I will always remember the way the crew acted after receiving this joyous news. They danced on the deck and some were singing. There was joy among our 130 crewmembers and the ship was still going through her punishment with the ice floes. We were now in what was called running ice, but we had drifted clear of the worst danger, the icebergs.

On the night of March 26, the lights of the *Sagona* were sighted from the barrel (this is on the masthead of the ship, better known as the crow's nest). She was sighted about 8 p.m. and at 4 p.m. the next day, after making her way through the heavy ice, the *Sagona* got to the disabled *Diana*.

The *Sagona* had been told to wait until she received orders from St. John's—whether she was to try and tow the *Diana* into port or take the crew off her. She received these orders the next morning and they were to sink the ship, as they could not tow her through the heavy Arctic ice. The *Sagona* was also instructed to take the seals off the abandoned *Diana*. This they started to do about 8 a.m. the following morning, but an unforeseen thing happened—the *Sagona* had only taken two hoists of seals on board when all of a sudden the *Diana* burst into a cloud of flames in the forward part of the ship. Yes, the *Diana* was on fire and all efforts to take the "fat" were abandoned by the *Sagona*.

The word to abandon ship was given to the *Diana* crew and everyone started going over the side of the ship, taking with them their sealing boxes, sea bags, and all their personal belongings. It wasn't long before flames had spread from the forward part of the ship to the after part and soon the *Diana* was in a mass of flames. It was a sight that will always be in my memory.

I watched her masts come tumbling down and her tarry punts burning in the davits. She burned to the water's rim, then what was left of her started to go down. As she disappeared beneath the waves, tears rolled down my cheeks, for she was my first ship.

The *Sagona* brought us into Bay de Verde, where we changed ships again and were taken to St. John's by a little ship called the *Watchful*. When we arrived back in St. John's, you can't imagine how glad we were and thankful to God that we had come through the ordeal.

The history of the sea is replete with stories told about different omens of bad luck. Among them is one that concerns a man that hard luck seemed to follow, as I was to find out later. We had such a man on the *Diana*. He made nine springs to the seal hunt and never collected a penny. The ships he sailed on were always out of money. I was surprised to find this man with us on this trip—this made 10 springs and the loss of a ship. If this is true, which a lot of people claim, it is a tough predicament to be in. However, there is such a thing as luck, and if it follows you it is a wonderful thing!

After we were landed on Queen's Wharf, the crew began to make their way up the street, for many of them had friends in St. John's. As for myself, I went with two of my shipmates to a place where they sold home brew. One of my companions was well acquainted with the place, which was called the Peephole in the Door. A fellow hauled over a slide and peeped out. My companion gave him the password, "Ship ahoy."

This was answered by the man inside who said, "Aye, aye, sir." Then the door opened and we went in where they sold home brew and moonshine. I did not have any of the moonshine, but the home brew I drank. It seemed to be quite good—my shipmates lowered down the moonshine as if it were skim milk.

The fellow who ran the place was a nice man and he seemed to make us welcome in every way. The moonshine was 20 cents a drink and the beer 10 cents a bottle.

While I was drinking my beer, a fellow started to sing "Spring of the Wadhams." It went like this:

I remember the spring of the Wadhams.
I sailed out in the brig called the Dan,
Maurice Crotty was one of our swoilers,
A comical, queer, funny man.

He sang songs and told stories forever,
His lies he could spin by the score,
When Crotty would strike up a ditty,
All the men in the galley would roar.

Chorus:
Tooral I oral I addy,
Tooral I oral I eee,
Tooral I oral I addy,
Tooral I oral I eee.

Oh, the day we sailed out through the Narrows
And the people were shouting on shore.
Crotty was filled with his sorrow,
For his girlfriends he had twenty-four.

Then down across Torbay we were steaming,
Headed out for the great white zone,
He said if the captain would land him
And he would call on the widow Malone.

After leaving this place, I took a stroll along Duckworth Street. I saw two girls coming toward me. One of them was Kay, who had come out from Torbay to meet me.

Now when a seal hunter came from the seal fishery, his clothes were all greasy and his face as black as coal, for a seal hunter never washed from the time he left until he got back. But when Kay saw me, she ran and grabbed me around the neck and I got a warm hug. Tears of joy were streaming down her face. I had never seen her act like this before and she really showed that she thought a lot of me.

We walked along the sidewalk until we came to a little restaurant known as Wood's Candy Store. All three of us went in and ordered a meal, and Kay told me about a dream she had had. I was surprised at how close this dream came to being true. She dreamed on March 17 that she saw the *Diana* out of the water on the ice with men running in all directions in confusion. The ship's foremast was broken and her lifeboats dangled from the davits. Then all of a sudden the ship burst into flames and burned to the waterline, whereupon she disappeared beneath the sea.

It was sad to hear the two girls tell how badly my father and mother felt about me, as there was no word from the ship from March 17 until March 25. This was a surprise because the ship had wireless, and therefore I thought she was in constant contact with her owners. This showed the stubbornness of the *Diana's* captain, who sent out no messages of the plight that we were in. If he could have reached land with the wireless or not, we never knew. No account of the mutiny that took place on board the *Diana* was ever published as far as I know.

St. John's at this time had Prohibition. There was a big change from the good old days when the saloons and drinking places were in full swing. As in the song of the Old Polina, there was plenty of gaiety and plenty of rum—and the rum was cheap. This was all gone and the old city looked as if a black cloud had come over the whole surroundings. But in the harbour there were many schooners that had come in from the bays to get supplies to carry to the Labrador, the shore fishery, and the Grand Banks fishery.

After visiting home in Torbay, I tried several times to ship on vessels that were going to Spain, Brazil, and different ports with salt cod, but all my attempts proved to be in vain.

I returned to Torbay, where we had some gay old times and dancing, and Kay and I were very happy. I think if I had taken her advice at this time my life would have been better and I would not have gone through all that I did in the years that followed. But I was really bent on going to sea and I could not content myself otherwise.

The weather in the early part of April was pleasant; the snow had all gone, and the rivers and ponds were like they are in the summer. One day Kay and I went for a picnic in the country. The place we chose for our picnic was beside a river that flows from Great Pond to Gosse's Pond. We were camped by the waterfall, where I used a rod and reel to catch a trout. These ponds were noted for rainbow trout but I didn't seem to have any luck catching one of them.

Just before sunset we witnessed a sight that I will always remember. The rainbow trout started to go up the river, jumping over the waterfall and landing on the top. The trout were very large. It seemed as if they curled themselves up like a hoop leaving the bottom of the waterfall and whirling themselves to the top. While this was going on, I landed seven lovely rainbow with my rod and reel. Getting a fighting rainbow on your hook is a challenge; he is more of a fighter than the Atlantic salmon.

We have 13 rainbow-stocked ponds in the Torbay area. These ponds were stocked with rainbow many years ago. They proved to be hard fish to catch with rod and reel. They feed mostly on leeches and they very seldom take worms. The best fly is the purple and red fly hook. They spend most of their time in the rivers. They leave the ponds in the morning at daylight and stay in the rivers until sundown. This is the best time to catch them, when they are returning to the pond at sundown and at daylight before they leave the pond; however, they can be taken throughout the day when they are in the rivers. They are about the best game fish in all Newfoundland, perhaps in the world.

CHAPTER 4

As I had no success in shipping out of St. John's, I decided to go to the United States. On May 18, I tried for transportation to Halifax and along with two more companions we sailed on the SS *Rosalind*, which was operating for Harvey & Company between St. John's and New York. This was the Red Cross Line. We sailed out through the St. John's Narrows in the late afternoon and the people were crowded along the Battery Road, cheering and bidding bon voyage to the ship as she sailed by the Battery and headed through the Narrows for the open sea. It was very hard for me to leave my little sweetheart, who was standing on the pier. I was overcome with a sorrow which I think only comes once in a lifetime, when you are leaving your native land for the first time. There's a little verse that goes like this:

My heart was sad, my tears were flowing,
My little sweetheart on the pier did stand,
I kissed goodbye, now I was going,
From the shores of Newfoundland.

My two companions and I were leaning over the rail. One of them seemed delighted to be going. His name was Michael Tapper of Torbay. The other man's name was Thomas Druken, and he was crying like a baby. When Tapper asked him what he was crying for, he said it was because his father and mother didn't want him to go. These two poor fellows never did return to Newfoundland. They both died in the United States, but I lived to return and see the homeland once more.

After arriving in Halifax we went to Yarmouth, Nova Scotia, where we had to pass the immigration people to go by train to Boston. But luck didn't seem to be with me, for when I arrived at immigration each one of us was handed a card to read. My two buddies read their cards, had no trouble, and passed through. When the immigration officer gave me the card to read, there was French on one side and English on the other. He passed me the French side. I was puzzled and could not understand a word. I thought this was what I had to read.

One would think that the immigration officer would have told me the difference. But he grabbed the card out of my hand and said, "You can't read; therefore you can't go."

"Oh, yes, sir, I can read," I said.

"You cannot."

Afterwards I found out what I was trying to read was French. After spending the night in the hotel in Yarmouth, I went down the next morning to the immigration office, where I got one of the cards, and, after looking it over, I found out my mistake. The English on the card was very easy to read. I then went to the officer again and tried to explain to him, but he was not very nice. He gave me no satisfaction and would not let me pass. I was turned down from going to the United States for a year. There was no use of my trying any further.

I decided to stay in Yarmouth and look for work. I had $100 in my pocket and I figured this would last until I could find a job of some kind. I bought a ticket on the train and went to Digby, where some lumber vessels were loading, for trade to the United States.

I first got work stowing lumber on the vessel, then when the vessel was ready to sail, the captain shipped me over as a deckhand. Her name was the *Evelyn*, with Captain Tom Scott of Lunenburg, and a crew of 10, who were all Nova Scotia men and the nicest shipmates I was ever with. I found that these Canadians really liked Newfoundlanders and there was nothing too much for them to do to help me. They always referred to themselves as Bluenosers—that was my first experience in finding out what Bluenosers really were. They were skilled seamen and displayed courage in danger and stormy weather on the high seas.

We left Nova Scotia on June 2, my birthday. I was headed out for the open seas and, as I think now, it was the start of my high adventures on the sea. When we arrived in the Bay of Fundy, we ran into a storm. It was the roughest weather I had ever encountered in my young life. We had a deck load of lumber that ran into thousands of feet, and in the storm we lost all of it. The *Evelyn* took a big beating in this storm and most of her sails were torn to ribbons. After getting her free from the tangle of lumber, we ran before the sea to the eastward to get in deeper water.

When we were running before the heavy seas and wind one night, it happened. We were off Cape Grand Mannan at the time. The night was as dark as ditches. The mate was at the wheel and I was standing watch on the forward part of the vessel. Without warning, the hoist rope on the outer jib broke and the jib went out around the bowsprit. The mate hollered to me to take the wheel so he could go out and try to save the jib, but I said, "I'll go."

I climbed out on the bowsprit, sometimes known as the jib boom. I climbed out alright and got hold of the piece of canvas that was going wild. I managed to get two lanyards around it to hold it in place.

On my return back to the deck from the jib boom, the vessel raised up on a big sea. Then she rolled over, dipping the jib boom under water with such a force I was washed overboard and the vessel passed over me. How long I was underneath the ship's bottom I don't know, but I surfaced and went astern in the vessel's wake. I was nearly gone and, with my heavy clothes, had all I could do to keep up. It was lucky for me I could do a little swimming, but with the long rubbers and heavy watch coat I found it almost impossible to stay afloat. Every now and then a big wash of water would break over my head and I thought this was the end of my life.

There was no sight of the vessel. All I could see was the angry ocean and the seas rolling in the darkness. The whitecaps looked like acres of white water. But I struggled for dear life, trying to keep afloat.

I think I was about to give up when out of the darkness a red light appeared, then a green light, and I knew the vessel had come around and was searching for me.

I found out after from the mate that they had quite a time trying to get the vessel around in the heavy sea and gales of wind, and they were about to give up the search for me when the mate saw my face in the glare of the red light. This is the starboard light on the rigging of the vessel. The brave men launched the lifeboat in the heavy sea and I was rescued. This was one of my close calls with death.

I was taken on board, but I was unconscious. After rolling me on the deck to get the water from me, they brought me down to the cabin and put me in the captain's bunk. The captain then poured brandy down my throat, and he afterwards said that every time he poured the brandy down my throat, I would throw up salt water. The cook said there was enough sea water in me to float a vessel, but I soon recovered.

The captain discovered that my watch coat was full of copper paint from the bottom of the vessel. The coat was torn down the middle where I was hooked for a while beneath the bottom. It was lucky for me that the coat tore down the back. If it hadn't ripped, I would never have gotten free from under her bottom.

In a few days I was about my work again on deck and none the worse for my adventure. It was about four days after that we arrived in Boston, where we unloaded the lumber. It was a significant loss to the owners, for the deck load of lumber was over 500,000 feet.

After leaving Boston, the *Evelyn* went back to Lunenburg to engage in more coasting activities, but here in Lunenburg I quit the ship and shook hands with my Nova Scotia shipmates and bid them all goodbye. I think it was about the hardest thing I've ever done, for I had grown to like them so well, as they were the best shipmates I had ever come in contact with.

From Lunenburg I went to Montreal and stayed in this city for about a week. This gave me quite a bit of time to look over the city, which I would class as one of the nicest in North America. It is made up of French- and English-speaking people and all with whom I came in contact were welcoming people.

After leaving Montreal I went by train to Boston. In Boston I met my two old buddies with whom I sailed from St. John's. They were now engaged in the fishing business, and it wasn't long before I joined a beam trawler. She was called the *Wild Goose* and was fishing out of Rockland, Maine. She had a crew of 18 men and captain and mate and she was a coal-burning steamboat.

Her crew was made up of Newfoundlanders, Americans, and some Irishmen. I think they were the toughest crew of fishermen I ever met, as I was to find out. All had spent time in prison, and some did time on Deer Island. They called it Deer Island down the bay, for this prison camp is located in Boston Bay. One had done time in Charlottetown prison, the house of correction in New Bedford, but all of the time served in prison was just for minor offences like drunkenness, fighting, and, in other words, disturbing the peace. However, they were all fine fishermen and also men who were good at drinking moonshine and any kind of alcohol they could find. They all had nicknames such as Buddy Tom, Fighting Jack, Roughneck Don, Hardboiled Smith, and Wild Dan O'Reilly.

My first day aboard the *Wild Goose* was in Rockland, Maine, and in the afternoon Wild Dan O'Reilly and Fighting Jack began fighting.

It was a real rough-and-tumble one and no one seemed to interfere. They beat one another up so much they could hardly stand after the fight was over.

That evening when we left Rockland, all the men were drunk and fighting. I was never so scared in all my life, and thinking any minute they would bang me with one of their haymakers, for a blow from one of these giants would certainly do bodily harm. There were many fights that evening in Rockland Harbour; everyone was drunk and I think the *Wild Goose* herself was drunk.

We were bound for the Grand Banks, also known as the Banks of Newfoundland or, to American fishermen, the Western Banks. Located about 90 miles south of Cape Race, Newfoundland, it is the world's greatest cod-fishing ground. There you will find trawlers from many nations. At the time we arrived on the Grand Banks there were 50 beam trawlers and 16 dory vessels, all of these vessels taking on board the plentiful codfish.

The *Wild Goose* had an otter trawl on both her port and starboard sides. One trawl was fished at a time. Attached to the trawl were two cables connected from the winch to the trawl net. It was set astern of the *Wild Goose*, 125 fathoms. It was kept open by two otter doors that looked like doors of a house, except that they were cased with iron bars. After the net is out for about an hour, it is hoisted back on board the trawler. Sometimes there was so much fish in the net that the deck would be full of fish, and you had hardly space to walk.

The work was very hard on the *Wild Goose*, especially the handling of the fish. Some of these large fish tipped the scales at 80 pounds and were heavy lifting for the fisherman. It was back-breaking work.

While we were on the Banks, we secured 340,000 pounds, which was a full load for the *Wild Goose*. We got very little sleep, for there were no watches. In those days a man had to stand and work until he fell down among the fish, exhausted. But the captain and mate did not have any feelings for the men of the crew. They just seemed to work them until they fell. Many a time on this trip tears were in my eyes when I thought of the happy home I had left back in Torbay.

On arriving in Boston, we landed some of our fish at Commonwealth Fish Pier. In those days there wasn't much of a market for fish, and we were sent to Gloucester to land some, then to Portland to land more. It took three days to unload the 340,000 pounds. Most of this fish was sold for a half-cent a pound, and when we went up to the office for our pay, we were all in for a big surprise. We were $9 in debt for our 340,000 pounds of cod and our two weeks' work!

I left the *Wild Goose* with not a nickel in my pocket. About a week after, I shipped on a dory vessel. She was called the *Baystead*, fishing out of Gloucester in command of Captain Picco. Again we sailed for the Grand Banks, this time in search of halibut. We had 12 double dories, two men in a dory. (A single dory has one fisherman on board.)

On arriving on the Grand Banks, we set out our trawls for halibut. Now this trawling is done on the southern part of the Grand Banks. The trawl starts from 15 fathoms of water and stretches out in 150 fathoms. There is an anchor on each end of the trawl. Sometimes the anchor on the southern end is in 200 fathoms of water. The anchor weighs about 15 pounds, and when the fishermen have to pull this anchor up in 250 fathoms of water, I think it's about the hardest work that ever a human being could do to make a living. But this kind of work went on for years by the Americans and fishermen who fished for a livelihood on the Banks of Newfoundland.

It was while fishing on the Grand Banks on this trip that my dory-mate and I had a very close call. We had just started to haul our trawl when the unforeseen mishap occurred. We had two halibut in the dory, weighing about 150 pounds each. I was hauling the trawl in at the time in the bow of the dory when this big halibut coming up on the trawl had to be taken off. It seemed to be about 200 pounds, and I told my dory-mate to lean over on the opposite side of the dory so that, in taking in the halibut, it wouldn't turn the boat over.

After balancing the halibut on the gunwales of the dory, I hit the halibut on the head with my club—a piece of hardwood—to kill it. When I thought the man was leaning over on the opposite side, I hauled the halibut over the gunwales. However, by the time the halibut was on the side of the dory, my dorymate slipped and fell over the same side. The dory overturned, dumping the two of us in the water. I managed to get hold of the painter end of the dory. This is a loop in the stem of the dory. After getting a firm hold on this rope, I managed to get hold of my dory-mate, who was no swimmer.

With the two of us holding onto the bow part of the dory, the dory started to go down head-first. After giving my mate a good firm hold on the loop, I managed to get around by the bottom of the dory and catch the loop that was sticking out of the plug in the aft end of the dory—this way the two of us held for dear life. There were no dories near us and our only hope was for the vessel to pick us up. As the vessel was some 5 miles from us, it was two hours before she finally sighted us. Captain Picco finally brought the ship to our rescue and my Nova Scotia fisherman and I were rescued. This was my second narrow escape in my early days at sea, and sometimes it kind of frightened me about going to sea again, but the sea seemed to be getting in my blood and I still kept on.

That was the only trip I made on a halibut vessel, and it lasted for about four months. We secured 180,000 pounds of halibut, which we landed in Boston. The share for the crew was $150 for five months of hard work on the Banks of Newfoundland. This will live in my memory until the end of my days.

I was now through with fishing for a while, at least. I looked around to get a steamship or a vessel that was going to foreign ports. (At this time rum-running was at its height.) I wanted to join a rum-runner; then one day my chance came. A shipmate of mine by the name of John Breen came to my room and said he had a job for me on a rum-runner. A friend of ours from Newfoundland was the captain. She was in Boston at the Atlantic Works, where we were supposed to join her. She was bound for Scotland for a load of rum, and we would get $500 for making the trip.

It didn't take me long to get my belongings together, and we both started off to the Atlantic Works, where the rum-runner lay. But on our way down Summer Street in East Boston with our clothes bags, we passed by a place that the fishermen called the Wine Jug. There was an Italian lady who used to sell wine there and was visited quite a lot by the fishermen. When we were passing the half-open door, I discovered two of the customers were former shipmates of mine. On seeing me going by with my clothes bag, one of them came out and invited me in for a drink of sour wine. I told him I did not have time to have a drink, and that we were going to join a vessel, but they would not listen and dragged me in.

My companion pleaded with me to come, as the vessel would be going out in half an hour and we would miss her if we delayed. I could not get clear of the fellows who had me by the arm, so I went in to the Wine Jug for the drink. We had a bottle of wine, and I did not want to leave without buying a drink for them.

Meanwhile, my companion waiting outside kept calling to me to come. How time flies in a place like this. You are talking about different things that happened on the boat and the time sure isn't long going. When I finally got away from them and made my way to the Atlantic Works, we discovered the vessel already had sailed and the two of us had lost our passage on the rum-runner with Captain Joe Bonia.

My companion was so mad at me for losing the passage that for a time I thought he would hit me. He was so mad that he left me, saying he would have nothing else to do with me. I did not see him anymore for a while because I shipped out of Boston, but we were to meet again.

The rum-runner went to Europe and, like many a ship, she never returned. She was never heard of and her fate is still unknown. So the bottle of wine had saved my life and also the life of my companion, Mr. Breen.

I spent quite awhile looking for a job in Boston. Then one day a millionaire's yacht came into Boston and in her crew were two Newfoundlanders whom I knew very well. I met them one night in Maverick House, a pool and billiard room on Maverick Square in East Boston. They promised to get me a job on the yacht that was going on a trip around the world. They were true to their promise, and the next morning I shipped out on the *Whirlwind*. She was a steamboat; in other words, a hard-coal burner. I signed on as a quartermaster for $100 a month. In those days this was big money for a sailor.

After leaving Boston we went to Nova Scotia, St. Peter's Locks, and visited many places around the coast of Nova Scotia. I think I had the best time of my life right here in this part of Canada. When we were in

Point Tupper, Port Hawkesbury, and many places around Nova Scotia, we used to be asked to dances on shore. We got to know many people and enjoyed ourselves tremendously with square dancing, Virginia reels, and the old reels. I don't think in all my travels that there was anyone who treated me better than the people of Nova Scotia.

After visiting many parts of Canada we sailed down to Port aux Basques, Newfoundland. After leaving Port aux Basques, we went down to the Straits of Belle Isle, visiting many small places, then down the Straits to Labrador to Goose Bay and on to Greenland. We had the best food and good accommodations, as the crew of the *Whirlwind* had the same menu as the millionaire himself.

On the *Whirlwind* we carried a party of 15 besides the crew. Some of these people were photographers, artists, writers, and so forth. The millionaire, Mr. Boland, was a wonderful man, and it seemed as if there was no treatment good enough for the crew of the *Whirlwind*.

On this trip we visited the island of St. Pierre, where we stayed for two weeks. There was plenty of champagne and all kinds of drinks in the French town. It is a beautiful place, and the hospitality of the people is second to none in the world.

After leaving St. Pierre, we went back to New York, where we stayed for a week, then headed south. We went into Moorehead City, Carolina, then to Georgetown, whereupon we turned back and went to Gloucester. In Gloucester two new double fishing dories were purchased. These dories were for landing in rough places which we had to visit. Little did I ever dream when I saw the new dories hoisted on board that I would use one of them to land on Cape Horn itself!

After leaving Gloucester, we returned to the coast of Newfoundland. This time we made landings on the Bird Rocks (southwest coast of Newfoundland) and on Sable Island. The place where we anchored was near what they called the North West Light. The lighthouse keeper told us that they had the records of 558 shipwrecks. It is sometimes referred to as the graveyard of the Atlantic. There were about 80 people living on

Sable Island at the time we visited there. We travelled over the island to see the wild ponies, which seemed to be numerous. We also visited the stockyards where they sometimes penned the ponies to capture them.

There are different shelters built all over the island that offered some protection against the cold wind and storms that sweep the island. It is a very barren place with very little brush, mostly sand dunes and shifting sand that sometimes would engulf a ship. Yes, Sable Island has the looks of a graveyard—the graveyard of the Atlantic!

The lighthouse keeper on a little island we visited in Newfoundland—I think it is called Bird Rocks—told me a story that happened there some years ago. He said a woman and a man were running the lighthouse and the last supply ship to visit the island would come in October. The woman's husband died in November, but there was nowhere she could bury him. She packed his body in salt and kept him until the supply ship returned in June, and all this time this brave woman kept the light going on the island until she was relieved by the new lighthouse keeper in June.

After visiting many ports in Newfoundland, Labrador, and Canada, the *Whirlwind* headed south again, this time down to the Falkland Islands. Many places in the Falkland Islands were visited, then my visit to Cape Horn itself.

Upon arriving at Cape Horn, we found it very rough. Although it was in July, showers of ice pellets were falling constantly night and day, and it got so rough at times we had to abandon Cape Horn and put to sea in deeper water.

We spent two weeks trying to get near the Horn, as the party was bent on landing a little westward of the Horn. There is a saying, "Wait for a time and you will get it." This proved to be true in our venture to land the parties near Cape Horn. That, I would say, was the most exciting part of my life at sea. The ship came within a mile of the famous Cape Horn itself. This was like a dream coming true, for all through my early boyhood I had heard the sailors talk about Cape Horn, and now on this morning of August 7 I saw Cape Horn in all her ancient splendour.

There was excitement on board the *Whirlwind*. Many people down through history have sailed around the Horn but very few had ever seen it from ships that passed that way. Most sailing ships gave Cape Horn a wide berth. It was called "running the easterly down." They would pass from 20 to 30 miles away from Cape Horn, and in this way they would never see it.

The SS Whirlwind *lying off Cape Horn, where Jack Dodd landed in 1923.*

The captain of the *Whirlwind* was a very careful man, and he kept the ship on the move all the time. He would not take a chance of anchoring in case of a storm that would come up suddenly and make it so rough in the shallow waters that the ship then would have quite a time getting away from there. Everything now was made ready for the landing on the northern part of Cape Horn.

We carried a motor launch which was about 85 feet long with a 15-foot beam. She was powered by a gasoline engine and had a cruising speed of 25 miles. She was lowered to the water and was in the command of the second mate, Mr. Bradley. The party going ashore was made up of a writer, an artist, a geologist, and two helpers. Then one of the dories was towed toward the northern tip of Cape Horn.

The launch towed us to within a quarter of a mile of land. This was about 10 a.m. I was put in charge of the dory and the party got on board the dory from the launch. I rowed them ashore, landing on a shingle beach about 3,000 yards from the tip of the Horn. The landing was made without much difficulty, although the surf rolling in on the beach looked worse than it was.

I got instructions from the party to wait while they scouted around on the land, taking notes and picking up different kinds of stones. Some still pictures were taken—we had no movie cameras with us.

We came back to the ship by noon; then another party was taken. This time we took the two dories in tow, landing the two dories on the same shingle beach, while the party again made the rounds of the island.

It was while waiting for the party that I decided to row down to the point of the Horn and try to land there. My companion, Eddy Divine, who was from Nova Scotia, said to me, "You shouldn't take chances on doing that because you may drown in your attempt to crawl upon the slippery rocks," but I had it on my mind to try it. Then Eddy said, "We will take one of the dories and I'll go along with you." So the two of us set out from the shingle beach and rowed down to the tip of Cape Horn itself.

Jack Dodd landing at Cape Horn, South America.

I would estimate that the long shaped rock, which is fairly flat, is about 6 or 7 feet high over the water. It resembles the back of a submarine running out from the highest land (which is about 70 or 80 feet high) and looks like Torbay Point in Newfoundland. This low part runs out about 2,000 feet. From the high land there is a formation of rock about the diameter of a barrel and stands about 10 feet high. It looks like it was shaped by human hands. It runs up about 6 or 7 feet, then has a turn like a cow's crumpled horn. This is the one they claim that gave Cape Horn its name.

Out about 500 feet in the sea there is another standing formation that looks like a swordfish's sword. It stands about 8 feet high and has no crooks in it at all. Then out into the sea about 300 feet from this one, there is another formation, about 10 feet high, about the size of a barrel in diameter, and has one turn in its top. This also looks like a cow's horn but is not as crumpled as the one farther inland.

Although the water was quite smooth and there was no wind, a heavy surf was rolling over the outer end of the Horn. You can imagine when the weather is rough and a strong wind blowing, this whole thing must be buried in under the waves that roll over it.

We tried several places to get a place to climb upon the whaleback of Cape Horn and we finally found a low place. Eddy, who was on the oars of the dory, backed it in to the rock and I climbed out of the stern and landed on Cape Horn. I had much difficulty climbing up the slippery rock that offered very few places for a foot- or hand-hold, but I made it to the top of the whaleback that the horns are fastened to. I walked in over the whaleback beam and put my right arm around the post that is called the Horn. After this I walked out on the rock to the part that is shaped like the swordfish's sword, but I could not get out to the outer one, as there was too much surf rolling over it.

I made my way back to the dory, where I found it was harder to get off the rock than it was climbing up it. Although it was only about an hour since I landed, it was quite rough and the dory kept jumping up and down and it looked for a while that I was trapped on Cape Horn.

Eddy said he would have to go back to the ship and get some help and also a life jacket for me, so that I could get in the life jacket and jump in the water. I was not a good enough swimmer to attempt it without a life jacket. However, this time he steered the dory to the rock and I jumped from the rock; I fell down in the dory and scraped my ribs on the right side. For a time I thought my ribs were broken, but after I came aboard the ship the doctor said nothing was broken, though my ribs were sore for a while after.

I had made my landing on the tip of the Horn, and it seems, as far as can be found out, that I am the only known Newfoundlander to have landed on Cape Horn, perhaps the only one of any country.

After our first day spent off Cape Horn, plans were made for another landing the next day, but this did not materialize. That night a storm came up and we had to get away from the shallow water of Cape Horn. Our parties were not satisfied, for they intended to land on all of the little islands. There are six of them in all and they are located in the vicinity of the Wollaston Islands.

After leaving the Cape, we steamed north to Isla Lennox, and anchored off there, where the water seemed to be smooth. It was while we were anchored here one night Mr. Boland sent down for me to visit him in his cabin. I was surprised in getting his message, for it was the first time he had ever sent for me. The first thing which ran through my mind was that I was in trouble because of landing from the dory to the Horn. On board the *Whirlwind* it was like in the Navy: everything had to be ordered by either Mr. Boland or the captain.

On reaching his cabin, I was received by his secretary, who guided me into his quarters. He was seated in an armchair, smoking a cigar. On seeing me enter, he got up and shook hands with me and then told me to sit down in the chair near him. As I sat down waiting for what he was going to say to me, I was surprised when he asked me what part of Newfoundland I was born in. I told him Torbay, near St. John's. He then said, "I suppose you have been a fisherman all your life."

"Yes, sir, I started fishing at a very early age." After explaining to him the kind of fishing I did in Newfoundland, I told him of my trips to the Grand Banks in American trawlers.

He was greatly interested in what I said, and when I would try to change the subject, he would want me to go on and tell him more of the fishing on the Grand Banks. I was asked many questions; then he surprised me by asking, "Where did you learn to figure out the weather?"

I kind of laughed and said, "Why, sir, I don't know much about the weather."

"Oh, yes, you do," he countered. "Mr. Bradley, our second mate, has been telling me all about it. Four or five different breezes of wind, we have already gone through, you had told him about before they happened. You also predicted 24 hours of fine smooth weather." This was the weather that we went by in our landing at Cape Horn. "What I want you to do," he said, "from now on, is to report to me the way you think the weather is going to act. I don't expect you to be correct all the time, but I know you have a talent for predicting the weather, and on this trip any forecasts we have obtained from land have never been right. You will be compensated for this at the end of our voyage."

After two or three drinks of good cherry wine, along with a couple of fine cigars, I left Mr. Boland's quarters to go down to the forecastle, where my shipmates were waiting and were very eager to know my business with the millionaire. I made no bones about it; I told them the truth. There was a little laughing done at first, and I had to laugh myself, but all of them assured me I could do it, that I would be more accurate than those weathermen on shore.

I don't know how I figured it out, but my first report to Mr. Boland was on August 15. I said, "There will be good weather starting on August 16. There will be a light southwesterly wind that will die away to a flat calm."

On August 16, the *Whirlwind* weighed anchor at Isla Lennox and again headed back to Cape Horn. By this time I had rounded Cape Horn back and forth six times. This was something which in my boyhood I never dreamed of that within two months I would round the Horn six times.

On reaching Cape Horn everything was made ready for landing on one of the other islands. True to my weather prediction, we had six days of calm weather and the sun was so hot that the temperature was 110°F at 5 a.m. All the landings were carried out in the same way, with the motor launch towing the two dories to within a quarter of a mile from the island. Then the parties were rowed ashore in the dories.

I know that a lot of pictures were taken, quite a bit of writing was done, and different kinds of plants, soil, and rock were brought back as samples. All this was of great interest to the parties concerned.

Life on board the *Whirlwind* with sailors and officers was really enjoyable and to me this adventure was all I had longed for all my young life.

I was keeping constant watch on the barometer. This is the glass that told us that when the barometric pressure was going down it was for stormy weather. A long slow falling pressure is the sign of a long gale of wind and a quick falling of the barometer is an indication of a short duration of wind. A barometer is something that needs a lot of study; you just can't look at a barometer and tell how the wind is going to be. When the barometer goes down to 29, you can have a hurricane or a twister or a gale-force wind. When this is going down, it's for westerly or northerly winds. The barometer going up to 35 and 38 is for easterly winds.

In my early boyhood, in studying navigation I got to know the barometer very well, along with another weather sign that appears in the sky, the moon, and even the trees. All help in figuring out the weather. This knowledge served me well, both in landing on Cape Horn and my trips around the world, and is still with me to this day.

After the great six days' calm at Cape Horn, I gave my second report to Mr. Boland. A change in the weather was indicated, as the barometer had started to fall. I knew we were going to have westerly winds. That night we hoisted our launch and our dories and got away from Cape Horn. This time we headed for a place to anchor. We had a wind that blew about 70 miles an hour. I was congratulated by Mr. Boland for the good weather we had off Cape Horn, and now telling about the big breeze really clinched it that I was pretty good on reporting weather. I was to go on reporting for our entire voyage, which lasted 18 months.

We anchored at a place called Hoste. It's about 60 miles from Cape Horn to the north. Farther along the coast is the sheep farm at Harberton. Some of the mutton produced on this farm was supplied to the *Whirlwind* and everyone enjoyed the fresh meat.

We stayed there for two days and then headed down to Sloggett, where we stayed two days more. In each place we got no shore leave until we came down to Pineto Espanio. Here we stayed for a week and shore leave was given. The people seemed to be very friendly, and everywhere we went we were met by kind people. They seemed to be made up of native Indians and quite a few different nationalities were in evidence. I must say that the girls were very beautiful and friendly to us sailors who were far away from home.

Once in awhile I thought of home in Newfoundland, my parents, friends, and my girlfriend, Kay. I wrote to her from Pineto Espanio, telling her it was no use to write me because I would not be there, as we were now going to Le Maire Strait and our next port of call was Cabo San Diego. Here we stayed two days and then down around to San Pablo, then through the Straits of Magellan to Chile, where we stayed for over a week. After leaving there we went to Punta Dungeness, then back again to Cabo San Diego, and, after leaving San Diego, we went back again around Cape Horn, where we ran into a big storm. This time the storm struck us hard and the *Whirlwind* really showed her fitness.

We had five casks of oil on deck, and while off Cape Horn the lashings on them parted and all five of the casks were loose on the deck. It was very dangerous work trying to lash them in the heavy seas. The seas were coming over the ship and filling her full of water from forward to aft. This wind is what they call a "Cape Horn Snorter."

As the ship was riding out the heavy seas, she had to be brought around and run before the seas, in order to get the casks that kept going back and forth on her deck, and already they had done quite a lot of damage to her bulwarks (her rails). The jolly boat that was on deck had all the sides busted in and everything in the dining room, which was on the first deck, was flushed with sea water. One of our lifeboats was smashed like kindling wood in the davits. Even up on the top deck the VIP quarters were full of sea water and there was confusion among everyone aboard.

After the ship was brought around and running before the heavy seas, we managed to get the five casks of oil back in their places and well secured. After all this was accomplished, we changed course and headed for Pineto Espanio, where repairs were made to parts damaged by the heavy seas.

We found life ashore very enjoyable and I guess all our ship's company enjoyed themselves. We were in the port one week when we had a change of plans. We went back to Le Maire Strait around Cabo San Diego, and then on to the Argentine ports and went around to Chile, where several more ports were visited. Then in the Isla de Chiloé the dories were again used to take parties ashore. We did put in considerable time in this place and some very interesting souvenirs were brought on board and many different kinds of plants, which our party seemed to be very interested in.

After leaving this port we went to Punta Catalina. This port is picturesque, a fine place for fruit and many kinds were taken on board. Then the long trip back to the United States was started.

CHAPTER 5

It took us three weeks to get back to Key West and we visited and explored from Key West to Barnes Sound. This was a real adventure for me, as I found every place so interesting.

As we made the trip from the tip of Key West, we visited many places. On one occasion we took on water and other supplies in a place called Boca Chica Key, then on to Sugar Loaf Key, and all along the stretch of connected islands. We made several landings, most of the time anchoring the ship. We went to Key Largo, where there's a small island standing off from the shore quite a piece. Right there, according to stories, was the wreck of the *Benward*. Now, according to our party, this ship had gone down with a lot of gold on board. We did a lot of cruising around this wreck. Many soundings were taken around what is known as Malaise Reef, and attempts were made to send down divers (we had one on board). In all the attempts we made in diving we were unsuccessful in obtaining anything of value, but we did get some pieces of the wreck that were good for souvenirs.

We spent considerable time at Key Largo, where we made quite a few landings on John Pennekamp Coral Reef Park. Our party seemed all excited after the visits they made here, where the statue of Our Lord is submerged 25 feet below the surface of the water. I did not get a chance to visit it myself, but apparently it shows Christ of the Abyss. Now this can be viewed through the bottom of the tourist boats. The bottom is glass and, on a good sunny day when the water is very smooth, it can be seen by leaning over the side of the boat.

This beautiful string of Keys was first found in the early part of the sixteenth century by a man named Ponce de Leon. The islands themselves are formed by limestone and coral that seems to be as hard as concrete. They are estimated to be 190 to 200 miles long.

On reaching the end of the Keys we then came back and went around Key West to Key West Island. We also made a landing on what is known as Boca Grande Key, then on Snipe Keys; then we went around to Johnston Key, and along our course to Pine Islands. This stretch of water had numerous small islands and is very hard to navigate.

But our captain was a careful navigator and took the *Whirlwind* all around to what is called Seven-Mile Bridge and then on to Fat Deer Island, where a whole week was spent along this stretch. We then went on down through Florida Bay, where we visited many places like Grassy Key and Duck Key.

After leaving this stretch of islands on the Florida coast, we visited Fort Jefferson. This fort was supposed to have had 135 guns. It became a federal prison and by all accounts the once-famous Dr. Samuel Mudd was a prisoner on this island for his connection with the assassination of Abraham Lincoln. There's a light on the wall on the southeast part of the island. This light was very useful in guiding ships that traded in this part of the world.

I landed on this island and found everything very interesting. The old place was first established in the middle of the seventeenth century, with a cost to the United States government of over $3 million. There is a good dock at the fort and a ship can get in easily without any fear of doing damage to its hull. We spent over a week at this place and made some trips around the prison walls and viewed many things of historic significance.

Our trip was coming to an end, and plans were under way to proceed down to the Panama Canal. Some talk was going on in the ship that we were to go around Cape Horn again. No one seemed to relish this, but as the days went by we were to visit Mexico City and make several landings along the coast of Mexico. You always feel joy on visiting a new country and view the ports for the first time. To me, the hours went by like minutes and the weeks were just like days.

After arriving in Mexico, most of the crew had shore leave and many drinking places were visited by the sailors. There were plenty of good drinks and plenty of charming senoritas.

After spending a week in Mexico City once again the lines were cast off and this time our course was set to the Panama Canal. As this was my first trip to the Canal, I was overjoyed and thought the ship wouldn't get there quickly enough.

On reaching Panama Bay, several interesting points were explained to us by our second mate, Mr. Bradley, who had been through the Panama Canal before. We visited a place called Colon. Right here is where they first tried to dig the Canal. This I understand was done by the French, who by all accounts spent $20 million, but it was unsuccessful and the project was abandoned by the French government. The French had the idea that by starting to dig the Canal in the low land they would have a better chance of success. But they were wrong. When the Americans started to build the canal, they picked out the highest mountain they could find. At this time a lot of people thought they were crazy to build a waterway through the high mountains of Panama, but they proved they were right, and after some unforeseen setbacks were overcome, the canal was built from the Atlantic to the Pacific.

After leaving Colon the *Whirlwind* steamed up to the entrance of the Canal to await her turn to go through. While we were waiting, we saw several ships going through. When a ship enters the first lock, she looks from the ocean like a statue that is hoisted up the mountain by an elevator. She seemed to stay there for a while and then disappeared; she had gone through the first lock. At last our turn came and we went through the procedure of entering the first lock and set down in the level water of the canal. Guide lines were put on board connected to both starboard and port sides of the ship. She was then towed along by small locomotives, one on each side of the Canal. Sometimes a ship could go through under her own power, but no chances are taken, as these lines are placed on her in case of mishap that could cause damage to the ship.

This is a breathtaking adventure, especially for one's first trip through the Canal. It takes roughly nine hours and it cuts off thousands of miles by not having to go down around Cape Horn.

Panama is a very exotic country. We visited Balboa. This is a lovely city and in some places on our way through we were showered with oranges—this was in the narrow sections of the Canal. The natives take pleasure in throwing oranges and other pieces of fruit on board the ships. This waterway is something one never forgets, and I think no one should die without having the adventure of going through the Panama Canal.

It never entered my mind at this time on my first trip that I would make nine passages through the Panama Canal and nine passages around Cape Horn itself, but in the days that followed I had the opportunity of making all these trips. The memories will be with me to the end of my life.

After the trip through the Canal we wondered where we were headed. These people did not make known their intentions to the crew of the ship, so you would just have to wait and see. Even Captain McLeod did not know all the time where the ship was going. To him it was like sailing under sealed orders. When the right time came, he was told the port he was to visit and the country. Then little bits of news would leak out through some conversation by the mate and captain and would fall on the ears of the quartermaster. However, on this occasion the news of where we were going had leaked out earlier than expected—we were bound for Australia!

We were to visit Sydney first, then Melbourne and other places that the millionaire had in his plans. As I was still figuring the weather forecast, I made many visits to Mr. Boland's quarters, and I became acquainted with his two daughters, Mary and Jenny. These two girls were very plain and, as rich girls, did not put on any show of being rich. In this I was surprised. They talked about the plain things of life. Their mother, who was with us now, was a nice woman. She liked to talk about her home in

Vermont, for, as she put it, there was no place like the farm in Vermont. She told me while in the United States she visited her home many times. This was her first adventure with her husband in so many different parts of the world, and she said she enjoyed it all tremendously.

Mr. Boland seemed to be more interested in the fishing out of Boston and Gloucester. It didn't matter what subject we were speaking about, he would always change it to some part of the fishing business. He was an admirer of Captain Bob Bartlett, whom he thought was the greatest Arctic navigator in the world. I know something about Captain Bob and had visited his birthplace, Brigus, Newfoundland. Mr. Boland had read quite a lot about Captain Bob, and the way he carried on the conversation was most interesting.

On her first few days out from the Panama Canal, the *Whirlwind* made good time. Her speed was 14 knots and the weather was really good, with plenty of sunshine and warm southwest winds. The crew rigged up a sunbath basket on the quarterdeck. This tub was made of canvas and was stretched from the lower part of the bridge to the fore-mast of the ship. It could hold 300 gallons of water and two or three persons could get in at the same time. The water was pumped into the bath by the deck hose. It was salt water, which sailors claim is good for the skin of the body and a protection against scurvy. If this is true or not, I don't really know, but one thing I am certain of: no one on the ship had any signs of scurvy or any skin blemish.

The nights were very warm and the beautiful moonlight with millions of bright stars was really good to look at. Up there in the clear blue heavens could be seen the Southern Cross that I had heard so much about back in my early boyhood days in Torbay. I was a long way from home and going further away every hour. I was thinking of my girl-friend, Kay, and wondering if I would ever see her again. I sometimes felt very sad and lonely when I thought of the gay times we had together.

The fine weather we were enjoying was short-lived. All of a sudden a storm was upon us. It started with a heavy rain and a gale of wind from the southwest. In no time at all the sea became so rough that the *Whirlwind* was swept from forward to aft by the high seas that rolled down on her. One of the seas smashed two of her lifeboats, took a piece of her outer bridge and made a wreck of it, also breaking all the glass in the pilot house. An awful lot of damage was caused to her main afterdeck. For 48 hours this wind lasted, blowing 80 miles an hour and gusting at times to 100 miles an hour. The ship was kept head to the wind with half speed in order to ride out the mountains of sea that rolled down on her.

After the storm was over, the *Whirlwind* was a shambles. A lot of damage was done to her top deck, but we were very lucky no damage was done to her hull and she came out of it with flying colours.

On arriving in Melbourne, Australia, we went to the shipyard for repairs. It took two weeks to get the ship back in shape, and it cost quite a bit of money, but it gave our crew plenty of time to get around in the city of Melbourne. We visited many places of interest, especially the beaches—and the drinking places. My thoughts went back to Newfoundland, especially Torbay, for it was on the south side of Torbay that Captain Cook landed his men in the attack on St. John's. Captain Cook was also the discoverer of Australia.

After leaving Melbourne, we went to Sydney, another prosperous city in Australia. In Sydney Harbour could be seen ships from many parts of the world under many different flags. It was very fascinating to see the way the ships discharged and loaded different cargoes.

We stayed two days in Sydney and our crew was wondering where we would be headed next. As we sailed out from Sydney, bits of news seemed to leak out. Then we found out where we were headed: New Guinea. When we arrived there, we visited two or three ports and then sailed to the island of Bali (famous for its beautiful girls). From Bali it was on to the rich and heavily populated island of Java. Here we visited many ports on the east and west coasts and found them very interesting.

A quick trip was made to Ceylon (for we were now in the Indian Ocean), and then we headed for the large island of Borneo. From there we went to the American-controlled islands of the Philippines. A quick trip across to Vietnam (French Indochina) and thence to the island colony of Hong Kong and we were headed for Japan.

We only visited one place in Japan, its capital, Tokyo. I was overjoyed on arriving in Tokyo, for I had dreamed of the island of Japan a long time ago. We found it a challenge to get around in the different dance halls and clubs, for it was very difficult trying to tell the Japanese what you wanted. I think at this time very little English was spoken in Japan, but we enjoyed the hospitality and learned how to get around. We found the Japanese people nice to deal with, especially the girls who would sometimes get us sailors out dancing, and it seemed they would spare no effort to make the strangers enjoy themselves.

When we left Tokyo, we headed for California. We arrived in San Diego a week before Christmas and spent the holidays there. For a while it seemed to us we would be staying all winter, but we left there January 11. As usual, we had no idea what country we were heading for. We passed the Panama Canal, and it became clear to us as we sailed along the west coast of South America that we were going to "round the Horn" once again.

On arriving at Cape Horn, we made several landings on small islands in the vicinity. After our party had carried out its explorations, we headed for the Mediterranean. We passed the Straits of Gibraltar, saw the Pillars of Hercules on our starboard bow, and visited ports in Algeria and the great port city of Barcelona, Spain. We called at Seville with its fine cathedrals and then went on to Lisbon, Portugal—we were leaving the Mediterranean now. Many fine ports in the Bay of Biscay were also visited.

The *Whirlwind* headed into the North Sea, calling at Copenhagen, Denmark, also Norway, Stockholm, and Sweden. After these places were visited our trip to Europe was cut short and we had to head back for the United States.

Our next port of call was the whaling port of New Bedford, Massachusetts. This once-famous whaling city seemed to be in a broken-down condition; the whaling business was pretty well gone and its docks were half rotten. Two of the whaling vessels were left at this time. One was called the *Wanderer*, which was still active in the whaling business. The other one was the *Charles W. Morgan*. The latter was afterwards taken over by the late Colonel Green of New Bedford. She was moored in a berth on Colonel Green's estate in south Dartmouth, where she was enshrined and placed on exhibition to be viewed by the general public. There is quite a bit of history attached to the Green estate. The colonel was very interested in collecting different items pertaining to the whaling industry and had many collections that were worth a fortune.

In New Bedford we visited the whaling museum, where can be found many interesting symbols of the bygone days of the whaling industry. In a building erected on Johnny Cake Hill, there is a whaling ship. You can see the dishes on the table as they were in the days of the industry. Here are the harpoons, whaling boats, and tub with the whaling line. There is everything in this museum from the days when the city of New Bedford lit the world in whale oil! You also can view the houses with their high attics with glass windows. According to the people, these were for watching the ships arrive. Now it was all gone but for a few small fishing boats that fished mostly Butler's Flats and the surrounding bay.

We wondered where we would be going next. At the present time we were visiting interesting places around Buzzard's Bay, such as Chuddy Hunt Lighthouse, Martha's Vineyard, Nantucket, and Edgartown. Those places were very famous in the days of the whaling industry. In the time of sailing ships, the cry of "There she blows" was very familiar both to the whalers and the people around New Bedford. Sometimes a ship would be gone four to five years.

While I was in New Bedford, I talked with some who had served time on whaling ships. One of them was Captain Silvary. He was still active and in command of the *Wanderer*. I talked with him four or five different times during our stay in port. He was a fine gentleman, and his stories were very interesting, especially his version of the shanty songs that were sung on the whaling ships.

SALLY BROWN

Sally Brown is a high-born lady
Hey ho, roll and go,
Roll and go, until she rolled me over,
Spent my money on you, Sally Brown.

She's a wee bit black,
But not too shady,
Hey ho, roll and go,
Roll and go, until she rolled me over
Spent my money on you, Sally Brown.

Sweet Sally got my four years' wages,
Hey ho, roll and go,
Roll and go, until she rolled me over,
Spent my money on you, Sally Brown.

This song was used when hoisting sails, anchors, and oil barrels and doing all the hard work on board ship.

JOLLY POKER

It's to my Jolly Poker,
We will hoist this heavy bugger,
And it's to my Jolly Poker haul.

Chorus
Haul on the bow line,
Heave and break the tow line,
Haul on the bow line,
Haul, boys, haul.

It's to my Jolly Poker,
Our old captain is a joker
And it's to my Jolly Poker,
Haul, boys, haul.

A PLACE ON JOHNNY CAKE HILL

There's a place in New Bedford
Not far from the pier,
Where they sell rum and whisky and beer.
There's a cute little barmaid,
And her name it is Lil,
And she is the rose of Johnny Cake Hill.

Chorus
To my bomp I adde,
Bump I adde,
Oh rumpty bump.

Right here I went drinking,
With a two-dollar bill,
And I married the barmaid
Upon Johnny Cake Hill.

According to the captain, these shanties were top hits of the whaling days. They were sung in many parts of the world where the sailing ships went in search of whales. His tales of the dangers that the men of the whalers encountered would give a person the creeps.

On the whale boat, all harpooners had to harpoon the great mammal of the sea. When the whale was hit, hounding and shooting through the sea, he invited potential danger to the crew. But still the undaunted men of New Bedford and Nantucket went on and on to search and conquer the whales of the seas.

The next plan our party had was a fishing trip, as I found out when I was sent for by Mr. Boland. I was told to visit his quarters on the guest deck, which was sometimes called the promenade deck. When I went up to his sitting room, I found him seated in a big leather armchair, smoking a cigar and wearing a big smile on his face.

On seeing me enter, he said, "Well, Jack, sit down. I want to have a little chat with you." Now this was about fishing off the United States coast, for we had planned such a trip. He said, "I first want to congratulate you on the weather predictions that have served us well on our trips around the world. And it was a pleasure to me and all my party. But we still have more countries to visit before we are through. You were 90 per cent right in your weather forecasting, and that is an excellent account. And I am very grateful to you. When the voyage is all over, I will see that you get paid for it as I promised.

"Now, we will talk about a fishing trip. It will be for one week. I want to go to Georges Bank and see for myself all the places I have heard about on this famous fishing bank. You know, it's sometimes referred to as the graveyard of the Atlantic. I have heard that many ships have been lost on the treacherous shoals. Now, as you have fished on Georges Bank on American trawlers, I understand that you know the shoals and where the worst shipwrecks took place and also where we will have to go to catch some fish. I want you to plan the places that we will have to go on the fishing ground. Will you do this for me?"

"I will do all I can to make the trip a success. But, sir, if I make some mistakes, you will have to put up with them. My experiences are limited."

He nodded. "That will be all right. You don't need to worry about them. We will sail on Monday, weather permitting." He then arose from the chair, filled up two glasses with port wine, and we drank a toast to our fishing trip to the famous Georges Bank.

I then left his quarters and went down to the forecastle and joined my shipmates. The men in the forecastle were having some fun. They had three guests from the shore who were being entertained by our crew, and they were enjoying the music of an accordion played by Freddy Newman, who was one of our crew and a real musician. He played Down East music, such as jigs, reels, and square dances, and American waltzes and the latest American song hits of the day. We all enjoyed a good time with the little brown jug on the table. The drinks went around and around. It didn't look much like Prohibition, but it was at its height in the United States at that time. And rum-running was at its peak. The rum-runners were much chased by the Coast Guard, both night and day; some were captured, but more got away. Now, that little brown jug was a native of St. Pierre and Miquelon. It was brought back by one of our crew when the *Whirlwind* visited that port in the early part of our trip. I guess we had more than one little brown jug on board. But it made no difference, as the Coast Guard did not bother the *Whirlwind*.

The sound of the Down East music made me feel homesick and my thoughts went back across the sea to my home in Newfoundland, to my friends, and my girl, Kay, whom I had not heard from for almost a year. There's nothing that can bring back memories like music, especially the tunes that one had grown up with from childhood.

The *Whirlwind* was now being made ready for our fishing expedition to Georges Bank; fishing lines, hooks and sinkers, jiggers, and also fresh bait were being brought on board. The bait was brought down from Boston. It consisted of frozen squid, mackerel, and herring. It was all stored down in the hold of the ship and put in ice to await our trip out.

Now I will explain some things about fishing tackle. A fishing line, sometimes referred to as a handline, is made of cotton material treated with a coating of steam tar. It smells like tar. As a lady once said, "I dearly love a sailor, but I hate the smell of tar."

The sinker, made of lead, is used to sink the line, with the bait and hook attached, to catch the fish. The hook has a barb like a flange, resembling that of a harpoon blade. The reel is made of wood and is used to wind the line on. The jigger is moulded out of lead and has a hook on each side; this also has a barb on each hook. When plunged into the fish's body, it holds firm, and the fish can't very well get off this hook. I will tell more about the jigger later, for it was with a jigger that we captured a man-eating shark. This was out on Georges Bank, when we made the trip. Steam tar, such as that on the fishing line, is also used on the rigging of sailing ships and sometimes on steamships. There's a song called "Yankee Man O'War" that refers to steam tar:

YANKEE MAN O'WAR

Young Susie was a pretty girl
Of valiant, brave and bold
And when young Susie joined the ship,
She was just nineteen years old.
She took a man's place,
But her sweet young face
Was dabbed with pitch and tar,
While serving in the Navy
On the Yankee man o'war.
She holystoned the deck, from forward to aft,
In wind and tempest cold, her hands so soft
But she went aloft, like a jolly sailor bold,
She done her part, right from the start,
Still all full of pitch and tar, young Susie did her duty,
On the Yankee man o'war.

She sailed the sea to China,
Where her life was not insured,
And little did young Willie think
That Susie was on board.
In the battle of Cuba
There she received a scar.
In the taking of Morro Castle,
On the Yankee man o'war.

Down on the deck,
Young Susie fell
In the midst of the ship's crew
Young Willie who was standing near,
To her assistance flew.
I wish it was me, instead of you,
Who did receive the scar.
My dear, why did you adventure,
On the Yankee man o'war.

On young Susie, Willie gazed,
In wonder and surprise
It was sad to see the briny tears,
Fall from young Willie's eyes,
I wished it was me, instead of you
Who did receive the scar.
Now behold your simple Susie
On the Yankee man o'war.

Back to New England they did go,
And they were married there,
The bells did ring,
While they did sing,
To banish every fear,
She sometimes speaks about the war,
When she received the scar.
When she fought beneath Old Glory,
On the Yankee man o'war.

As we all know, many fine songs have come from the American struggle for freedom and independence on land and sea.

CHAPTER 6

When all was made ready for our fishing trip, the *Whirlwind* set sail from New Bedford. She steamed out of the harbour past Butler's Flats light, at the entrance of New Bedford Harbour. The sea was very smooth as we steamed up the channel to the *Hen and Chicken* lightship. The *Whirlwind* drew too much water to go through Woods Opening, which was sometimes called a hole, and couldn't go through Quick's Opening either. After passing by the *Hen and Chicken* lightship, we headed across to Block Island. But we changed our course to eastward before reaching Block Island, which course would take us down to Vineyard Sound, near Nantucket Island. The well-known island called No Man's Land was really worth looking at; also the many wooded places on the Woods Hole side.

As we steamed along, our party had a good view of the highlands of Hyannis. There were many fine buildings and yachts in the surrounding vicinity. We passed by the *Half Moon* lightship, the *Crossrip* lightship, and the *Handkerchief* lightship. We then set our course to Public Rip Channel. On reaching this channel we set our course to the *Nantucket* lightship, which was sometimes called the *Southshore* lightship. We had now passed five lightships and were heading for the sixth. They were all within a distance of 40 to 60 miles.

After reaching the *Nantucket* lightship, the *Whirlwind* was then put on a course to Georges Bank. We arrived there just about daybreak the next morning. We went as close as possible to the cultivator shoal, meaning shallow water. The ocean was calm, but the rollers were still going over the shallow place. It resembled a great surf on an open beach. Our party was overjoyed to see the cultivator on the much-talked-about Georges Bank. I was also fascinated by being so close to the shoals.

In years gone by this dreaded place of shallow water had taken the lives of many fishermen. It is sometimes referred to as the graveyard of the Atlantic Ocean, and I wrote a song about it entitled "The Vessel *Morning Gloom*." This was the name of one of the vessels that had come out of a storm at a time when so many vessels were lost. She lost over half her crew in her battle with the seas on the cultivator shoals.

The story was told by one of the *Morning Gloom* survivors. There were 22 fishing vessels lost at the time of this hurricane on Georges Bank, in the early 1800s. How many men lost their lives is not really known, but it's estimated at 20 men for each vessel. It caused a lot of grief and tears to the families of Gloucester, Boston, and Portland, but most of the men were from Gloucester. There is a day in Gloucester when the people throw thousands of bunches of flowers on the water of the harbour in token of the fishermen who lost their lives at sea. My song about the cultivator shoal goes like this:

THE VESSEL *MORNING GLOOM*

Her name it was the Morning Gloom
She sailed from Gloucester town,
And many friends waved them goodbye,
When she was outward bound.
Her sails were like the falling snow,
And she looked so neat and trim,
A Gloucester man was in command,
His name was Captain Jim.

No thought of danger was in their minds,
As they hoisted on all sail,

And the Morning Gloom, *she sailed along*
Spanked by a northeast gale.
She could outsail a clipper ship,
As she sailed away from shore
And for many of her crew on board,
They would see their homes no more.

They anchored on old Georges Bank,
Near the cultivator shoal,
Where many a gallant fisherman lay,
Their faith still lived untold.
Many vessels were anchored there,
And there seemed to be no room
It caused a lot of discontent
On board the Morning Gloom.

We were not long at anchor,
Just near the break of day,
Our captain now, aloud did shout.
"A storm was on its way."
The wind and sleet,
In this dreadful storm
Caused heavy seas to roll,
And for this great scrape,
There was no escape
From the cultivator shoal.

It was by kind providence,
We were just in time
We cut the cable from the bow,
And left the shoals behind.
Many vessels of the noble fleet,

Were sinking all around.
And twenty-two, with all their crew
On Georges Bank went down.

We tried her under double reef sails,
But not much could she do,
Our captain he gave orders
His voice was loud and true
"Shake out all reefs,
Trim half your sheets,
The shoals we must keep clear."
And for twelve long hours,
On a bow line stretch
Through the waters she did tear.

To see those sinking fishermen,
As we did pass them by
All clinging to the battered wrecks,
And loud for help did cry.
No help could we offer them
But we hoisted on all sail,
And like a frightened albatross
She raced before the gale.

Out of our crew of twenty-two
I'm sorry to describe,
Most of them were swept overboard,
Only six now survived.
It's sad to see your shipmates
Swept to a watery doom,
The noble men, who sailed from land
On the good ship, Morning Gloom.

This dreadful sight on Georges Bank,
Will be with me through the years
I fancy, I can see them now,
And their cries ring in my ears
It often does run in my mind,
I think I see them yet,
For what happened there on Georges Bank
I never will forget.

Thanks to the great Almighty God,
Some way we did come through,
To live with all my memories
Out on the ocean blue,
And thanks to our brave Captain Jim,
Who saved the ship from doom,
Commander of that noble ship,
The glorious Morning Gloom.

The vessel *Morning Gloom* is supposed to be the only vessel to survive the storm on Georges Bank. With most of her crew washed overboard, she kept on running before the heavy storm until the light on Cape Race, Newfoundland, was sighted. This light had three white flashes, which the captain of the *Morning Gloom* was well acquainted with, and it was really a cheerful sight to all his crew.

As described by one of the crew members in later years, they had to keep running before the wind and sea. It was too dangerous to "bring the vessel to" in case she might founder or be dismasted. They kept on going before the heavy seas, and they claimed the wind was 90 miles an hour at times, gusting to 100 miles an hour!

On arriving in St. John's they were greeted warmly by the Newfoundland people, who offered them assistance. No stone was left unturned to help the American crew. As one of the crew members said about the people of Newfoundland, "We were treated kindly by our Newfoundland friends."

With kind heart and hand,
And I won't forget
While I have breath,
Our friends in Newfoundland.

As we were here to visit the cultivator shoals in the *Whirlwind*, precautions had to be taken by our captain for the safety of the ship. We sailed looking at the seas, now rolling over this stretch of shallow water. There was no wind at all, and I wondered what it must have looked like in a 90-mile gale. For sure the seas must be like mountains. But we kept a safe distance from the breakers and sounded as we went.

The sounding was done by hand. The sounding lead weighed 10 pounds, attached to a strong 16-pound line, and for the man sounding it was not an easy job. The lead had to be thrown every two or three minutes in order to tell the depth of the water.

We stopped in different places along the shoals and put out our lines to catch fish. In this we were very successful, for we caught about 50 or 60 haddock, and also two chicken halibut, which were received with high honours by our party. A chicken halibut is a young halibut, weighing from 10 to 25 pounds, and is very delicious either baked, boiled, or fried. Many of our party had never seen handlining done before. They all seemed to be excited and everyone was taking part in catching the fish.

One of the men was using a cod jigger and he contacted a shark. It took two men to pull it up to the side of the ship, and there were times when we thought the hooks of the jigger would pull out of the shark's body. We were later to find out that the shark had the jigger in his mouth; he had swallowed the jigger, thinking it was bait. But the hooks held firm and the great man-eating shark was hoisted on board the *Whirlwind*. Its colour was light grey and it measured 15 feet from the tip of its nose to the tip of its tail. Its nose was rounded like a shovel, which is why it is sometimes called a shovel-nose shark. It had two rows of teeth—these teeth are about a half-inch long—and eyes about the size of a golf ball. It was a fearsome-looking creature and it would give anyone the creeps to think of being attacked by this monster in the water. After pictures were taken, the shark was hoisted up by the tail and thrown over the side.

After cruising all around the shoals, we headed for what is now called the north shoal. This is located on the eastern part of Georges Bank, and, like the cultivator shoal, it is always rough and very dangerous to shipping. It stretches across from north to south roughly 2 miles long.

After four days of cruising on the Bank, we steamed to the Flemish Cap. After spending the next two days on the Flemish Cap, we did some more handlining and caught more fish. We sighted four trawlers fishing there, also two dory vessels with their trawls set out. All of this was interesting to our party and most of our crew. After leaving the Flemish Cap, we set our course for the Grand Banks.

When we arrived on the Grand Banks, we found we had plenty of company. We counted 58 otter trawlers, sometimes called beam trawlers. To make it plain to the readers, a trawler is a small ship, approximately 100 to 200 feet long, about 20 feet wide, and sometimes powered by steam or diesel engine. The fishing nets that are dragged by the trawlers are called otter trawls or dragnets. There are two wire cables attached to doors: they look like the doors of a house and they are cased with iron bands. They are called iron shoes and are on the bottom part of the door. The weight helps to keep the doors down on the ocean bottom. Each door is called an otter board, and each otter board has a cable attached to it. This cable leads from the board to the net. The two otter boards are used to keep the net open when it is being dragged along the ocean floor. The net has a wide-open mouth that is formed like a circle; this is where the fish enter the net. In order to keep the net open, the boat must be travelling at a speed of about 5 or 6 miles per hour.

This type of boat, called an otter trawler, is much the same design as a dragger, but draggers are much smaller. There were other vessels fishing on the Banks. Some were fishing for halibut and more for codfish and haddock. All the ships were from different places, including France, Germany, England, Belgium, and Norway.

It was a most interesting sight to view the dory fishermen setting their trawls. They set with the tide, and if the tide is going to the south, they set south. If the tide is going to the north, they set to the north. In other words, they set their trawls the way the tide is running.

The Grand Banks is famous for codfish, halibut, and haddock. To the southeast of the Grand Banks is the deepest water in the Atlantic Ocean. The water is over a mile deep. (Some say there are 3 miles of water.) It is not the deepest water in the world, for they claim in the South Pacific they have found water 8 miles deep!

It is claimed that Christopher Columbus on his voyage to the new world first took a sounding on the Grand Banks after missing Newfoundland by a close margin. It was here that Columbus picked up a spruce tree that gave him an idea that land lay to the west of him and really gave him new hope that he would make a discovery. When the tree was examined on board Columbus's ship, it was found that the trunk was burned off instead of being cut off. Columbus knew that the stump and roots of this tree were still on land somewhere! It looked to all the men on Columbus's ship that whoever had burned this tree off had no tools to cut it. Therefore, this must have been done by Indians somewhere on the island of Newfoundland, where white spruce trees are plentiful. The Indians used the bark of white spruce to make medicine, a remedy which is still used today.

The Grand Banks is very cold in winter. The weather is more severe than it is on Georges Bank, but it is not as dangerous in stormy weather as is Georges Bank. There is no record of a great loss of life on the Grand Banks as there is on Georges Bank. And greater numbers of ships fish on the Newfoundland Banks than on Georges Bank.

In 1888 the dory vessel *Jubilee* out of St. John's, Newfoundland, lost two men in a dory in a thick fog. The captain of the *Jubilee* searched for five days for his missing men, but when he found no sign of them, he returned to St. John's with his flag at half-mast, and the two men were given up for lost. But an old slogan goes, "There's hope from the ocean, but none from the grave," and this proves true in this particular case.

The two men were Edward and Peter Flanigan. They were brothers and had been born in Torbay, Newfoundland. When they first got lost from the vessel the first night, they did not think they were astray. They kept on rowing until about midnight, when they got into ice floes. There were times when they had to pull the dory up on the ice pans. It was quite cold; the wind was northeast, blowing about 30 to 40 miles per hour, with showers of snow.

The Flanigan brothers spent the whole night battling with the ice floe, trying to save their dory from getting crushed in the ice. At the break of day they managed to get their dory free of the ice jam and once more were in open waters. After the terrible ordeal they went through, the brave men still held out hopes that they would be picked up.

Peter, who was the older, had all his fingers frostbitten. The agony he was in was so severe that he lay down on the bottom of the dory and there he stayed, sick from the pain of the frostbite. His brother, Edward, tried in every way to convince him to get up, but to no avail. After four days he was still lying there. Edward thought his brother had died, for he could not detect any life in his body. He took off his own oil coat and placed it over the body; then he took the trawl lines from the tubs and piled them all on his brother's body, thinking at this time that he really was dead.

This went on for over 11 days. He rowed sometimes as the dory drifted around, until he finally became so exhausted that he lay down to die. He lost consciousness on the eleventh day, and on the twelfth morning they were picked up by the vessel *Jessie Morrissey*, in the command of Captain Marly, on her way to Canada from Europe. Now this rescue was a genuine miracle, for the *Morrissey* picked them up in a thick fog. They were right in the vessel's course, so close that it almost ran the dory down.

After the dory was hoisted on board the *Morrissey*, it looked to all the crew as if there was just one man in her. They took the man that was unconscious and put him in a bed and tried to revive him. Then the captain told the crew to take all the gear out of the dory. To their surprise, they discovered another body lying underneath the trawl lines. They could not detect any signs of life in this man, but he was also placed in a bed down in the cabin. With the aid of some of his men, the captain tried to revive him.

As the story goes, for eight days Edward Flanigan thought his brother was dead and at times it occurred to him to put the dead man overboard, but then he changed his mind and let him stay. But the last man, Peter, whom they thought was dead, was the first one to show signs of life, and he regained consciousness four hours before Edward!

When Edward regained consciousness, he was told he was on the vessel *Morrissey* on his way to Canada. It seemed to cheer him a little at first; then he said to the captain, "My poor brother, Peter. He died. Did you see him?"

Then the captain said, "Now, Edward, I've got good news for you. Your brother is not dead, but much alive. He is down in the next berth and wants to talk to you."

It wasn't long before the two were talking to each other and, in spite of Peter's frozen fingers, which still caused him considerable pain, they were soon laughing.

They had lived 12 days and nights without food or water, thereby writing a page in Newfoundland history. They were landed in Quebec, where they recovered and then were sent to their homes in Newfoundland, where they lived for many years after. But they never sailed to the Grand Banks again! A song was written about them:

THE GRAND BANKS FAR AWAY

Oh, my thoughts go back in song and story,
Of the gallant men, the Flanigans from Torbay,

Who survived for twelve days in a dory,
Adrift on the Grand Banks far away.
The Flanigans were the bravest of the brave,
No greater seamen ever sailed the sea,
The children should read of them in story,
A symbol of Newfoundland history.

After leaving the Grand Banks, the *Whirlwind* went to Halifax, Nova Scotia. At this time in Halifax, they were clearing away and rebuilding after the great explosion back in the early part of First World War. After the *Whirlwind* was tied up in Halifax, we were given plenty of shore leave and our party visited many interesting places of Halifax history, including a visit to the rose garden park.

I think this was the loveliest display of roses and different varieties of flowers I had seen in the many countries we visited. Halifax is an unusually beautiful city and the people are second to none. Their hospitality and their warm welcome to a visitor are outstanding. The stranger is always welcome and is treated with kindness.

Our party paid a visit inland from Halifax to see the anchor that had been driven about 2 miles inland by the impact of the explosion. The anchor, weighing 1,000 pounds, was thrown from the waterfront over housetops and treetops.

After supplies were taken on board we left the port of Halifax, and, to my surprise, and the surprise of all the crew, we were headed once more for the island of Newfoundland, this time to the west coast, where we visited Port aux Basques. Our party again went ashore and we were given shore leave on our first day in port. That night the people of Channel gave us a dance, which was held in a kitchen. This is sometimes called a "kitchen racket." The music, supplied by an accordion and a fiddle, has been played for years in Newfoundland, not only for square dances, American eights, lancers, and waltzes but also for jigs and reels. One lady got out and danced what she called the sailor's hornpipe. She was about 70 years old and I think she was more supple on her feet than a young girl of 16. We enjoyed ourselves tremendously at this fine Newfoundland dance in Channel. We went on board our ship with happy memories.

The next morning the *Whirlwind* weighed anchor and headed out through the Gulf, this time down through the Gulf of St. Lawrence. Our next port of call was Corner Brook in the Bay of Islands. Corner Brook was not much more than a railroad town, where there were some sawmills and several schooners loading lumber.

There were quite a few two-masted vessels in the lumber trade at this time, for lumber was a good business in this west coast town that was to become the site of the largest paper mill in Newfoundland. The fishery was carried out in a large-scale operation, and it seemed that the salmon and herring fishery was the main industry in the Bay of Islands. The black smoke of the Newfoundland train could be seen all along the waterfront. The train was called the Overland Express and in future years she was called the Newfie Bullet.

Corner Brook is a most breathtaking place with its towering heights, rocky mountains, hills, valley, and a harbour that offers security and safe protection for all shipping. The famous Humber River flows down along the Humber Arm and beautiful scenery is to be found all along its banks. Here can be found good salmon fishing for the interested sportsman. There are camping grounds all along the river, and where the Humber meets the sea, you will find good commercial fishing. The species of fish are halibut, codfish, lobster, and flounder of different types. The herring fishery is also carried on by the plants in Curling and surrounding places in the bay. The fishing is done in both summer and winter, for in the winter the fishermen cut holes in the ice to put down their nets and run them along underneath the ice.

Our party went up the Humber Arm, taking along with them camping equipment and enough provisions for a week's fishing and sightseeing. They afterwards said that they enjoyed themselves on the Humber River more than they had in any other part of the world.

While they were gone on their expedition up the Humber River, I decided to take a trip on the Overland Express. The mate told me I could have four days off. This would give me time to visit Millertown, for I had written a song about this lumber town, although I had never seen the place in my life.

When I arrived at the railroad station, the place was full of waiting passengers. It looked like the Overland Express would be crowded and it showed a thriving business for the railroad, which at this time was operated by the Newfoundland government. After getting my ticket, I did not have to wait long before the famous little train came rattling and puffing into the station. She had such a black smoke that coal fumes were all over the place.

After getting on board I took a seat in the first-class compartment by an old gentleman who greeted me with a cheerful smile. He was most friendly and began talking right away. He spoke quite plainly and his words had a touch of the bay in them and also a touch of Irish. I asked him where he was going, and he smiled and said, "All the way," meaning to St. John's, for that would be the end of the railway line. Now that I had a companion for quite a piece of the road, I started asking him some questions.

He said his age was 82, and he lived in Corner Brook. He had spent all his life along the railroad, when it was being built and afterwards. He was a steam locomotive engineer, retired from the service some years before. Now he was travelling on a free pass, which he could use on any branch of the rail line. I asked him how he liked riding on the train, and he smiled and said, "I like it very much, and I enjoy every inch of the trip, I've been on the Overland Express so long that I feel the train is a part of me and I'm a part of her."

There seemed to be a touch of sadness in his voice when he mentioned days gone by. He said they had their ups and downs, hardships, hard toil, and many inconveniences, but, he said, "They were still the good old days when I was a young fellow working on the railroad. I helped to build this narrow-gauge railway from St. John's to Port aux Basques, and we suffered hardships from cold in winter and from heat in the summer time. The mosquitoes were numerous all along the right-of-way. There were many places where some of the workmen were so severely bitten by mosquitoes that they were deadly sick and sometimes died with fever. We had no protection from the mosquito bites, for there were no doctors and very little medicine for protection against illness.

"There's a place along the track that I will always remember. It's called Jumpers Brook. It was here by the river where the workmen would take off their jumpers before going to work and hang them on the trees. Most every workman wore a jumper in those days. The jumpers were made of a lightweight, white canvas. Along by the brook were several big fir trees, also some birches. When a workman took off his jumper, he hung it on the limb of a tree. Sometimes there were so many jumpers there was no room for any more, and it wasn't long before the place was referred to by the workmen as Jumpers Brook. A railroad station was built there and the conductor on the train would shout, 'Next stop, Jumpers Brook.' It's located between Bishops Falls and Norris Arm."

He went on to relate that along this river were built many so-called camps for the workmen. Each man had to prepare his own camp. They were made with sticks and boughs, with no floors. The roof was covered with rinds and there were plenty of leaks in the camps. Rinds are the bark from trees. It is peeled off in one piece, and it looks like a strip of felt. They were so cold in the winter that you would have to sit up all night and keep a wood fire going to keep warm. They had no stoves, and the fires were mostly outside; as time went on some kind of stove was set up. The men mostly used boughs for mattresses and sometimes bunks were rigged up with the bottoms made of rope strands. The cookhouses were built with logs, which were stuffed with moss, on the sides of the camps.

The food was very rough, like salt beef, pork and beans, and hard tack, and it was very seldom that the cook made bread or any kind of cake. The tea was called switchel tea and sometimes juniper tea was used. Coffee was unheard of at that time. The men worked like horses, and the work was always back-breaking: cutting the right-of-way, digging through rocks, and pulling up tree stumps. The pick, shovel, crowbar, and wooden pliers were the main tools used on the railroad at this time. The workday was 12 hours and the average pay per man was $1.50, approximately 12.5 cents an hour! Still there were men coming from all over Newfoundland in search of work on the railroad.

After a hard day's work it felt good to lie down on a cozy bed of green boughs. The men were so exhausted that they went to sleep like newborn babies. The old man said, "We were sometimes awakened by the rain falling on the roof; this caused leaks, and we would have to get up and put on our oil cloths and stay up all night. But if the night was fine, we were in for a good night's sleep. We had some entertainment, for a fellow played the accordion and another played the fiddle. They played jigs and hornpipes and this cheered the workmen up a bit, as some of them were far away from home. We also had a Scotsman who played the bagpipes.

"On one occasion, some of the workmen's wives came in from the east on a flatcar and brought some more girls with them. We had a dance in the cookhouse. The dance floor was not a very good one, for it was made of huge sticks of wood with the rough knots all over it. But the boys and girls all seemed to enjoy themselves dancing to the music of the accordion, fiddle, and bagpipes. The women wore long dresses that swept the floor. The men were dressed in coveralls and some of them wore whiskers. It was the first and last dance we had along the railroad now known as the Jumpers Brook Line."

My companion was well acquainted with the building of the railroad across the wilds of Newfoundland. He gave me a correct account of the construction of the Newfoundland Overland Express. He said it was a big blunder on the part of the designers and planners from the start. He said it should have been a standard gauge and have followed a straight route. The Newfoundland Railway was more like a snake path than a railroad. It was built from St. John's east to Port aux Basques, with many branches which proved very serviceable to the people of the bays of Newfoundland. Now, as the old man was a railroad engineer, he could really tell the wrongs and faults on the railway line.

He said it was impossible to get speed over the crooked narrow gauge; there were places along the line where the engine of the train almost did the loop, the engine nearly meeting the rear car in a circle. I asked him why he did not like the narrow-gauge track, and he said, "A narrow track has so much vibration in it caused by the heavy rolling stock going over it that the vibration causes the road bed to crumble and sometimes cave in. This caused numerous derailments, many injuries, and loss of life. A wide track has less vibration and stands up more firmly, with fewer derailments and is safer in every way.

"I am looking ahead to the day when a real good train transportation system crosses the island of Newfoundland, with a standard-gauge rail and a straighter railroad that would cut miles off the distance and would be more up to date for the people of Newfoundland."

The first survey of the railroad was made in 1875 and, like all Newfoundland projects, it took a long time for it to go through. It took 35 years to complete. It got off to a slow start in 1881; by 1888 it was as far as Whitbourne, and then the company failed. In 1891, they started again and went as far as Trinity and Bonavista bays, and then in 1894 the banks lost their money and the railway failed again. Finally in 1896 it as put through to Port aux Basques, where the last spike was driven in the famous narrow-gauge rail on the barren flats. A year later, an agreement was made with Canada to run passenger ships across the Gulf of St. Lawrence. The railroad was operated by the Reid Newfoundland Company, who ran it until 1923. Then it was taken over by the Newfoundland government.

During the Second World War, the Overland Express got the name the "Newfie Bullet." This name was given by an American base worker who asked the conductor, "What time will this bullet get into St. John's?" So from then on she was known as the Newfie Bullet.

I had my lunch in the dining car and I was surprised to see that this diner was really up to date. There were nice linen cloths on the tables, and the waiters wore white coats and were spotlessly clean. The dining cars on the Newfoundland train are famous for their good cooks and delicious food. I sat at the table and, on looking over the menu, I noticed there was Newfoundland salmon for the specialty of the day, so I ordered some. This meal was served with French-fried potatoes, green peas, and a delicious sauce. I enjoyed it immensely, for it had been a long time since I had eaten fresh salmon. In many places that I had been around the world I had heard Newfoundland salmon mentioned, but it is mostly referred to as Atlantic salmon.

We passed through Bishops Falls, then through Jumpers Brook, and I had time to get a look at the place that was I was becoming very interested in. The old man and I got off the train, where he pointed out a few interesting things to me. Our stay at Jumpers Brook was short and we were on our way again. I won't go into full detail of the places we passed through, but we did have a one-hour stop at Howley. After leaving Howley, we went over the famous Gaff Topsails, 1,600 feet above sea level. You could look down on the valleys and ponds below. It's all very beautiful and my friend claimed that the ponds were full of trout.

The train seemed to crawl along very slowly making this upward grade; it was a hard climb with her two coal-burning engines, which sent clouds of black smoke all over the place. Therefore, I had a chance to view what is called the Topsails. There are three of them and they run from 200 to 300 feet high. Why they gave these hills the name of Gaff Topsails, I can't understand, for they don't look like the topsails of a ship in any way. They look more like domes, and they are different from any hills I have seen. Caribou could be observed in many places along the railway going over the Topsails, four or five in a little band, and they were very interesting to watch. The land all along the Topsails is very rocky, just scrub and brush, and it's really a rough terrain.

After going over the Topsails, we finally arrived in Millertown. As this was my destination, I shook hands and said goodbye to my friend, for we were never to meet again. Millertown was a nice place with piles of logs all around and busy sawmills. It is famous for its lumber industry and its lumberjacks. As I said before, I had written a song about this town, which I had not seen at the time.

I was overjoyed to be in this town that I had heard so much about. And all these lumberjacks were going by with their double bitters, and cries of "Timber! Timber!" were to be heard all over. I found myself a boardinghouse and put up for the night. I was very lucky, for that night they had a dance at the boardinghouse. About 8 p.m. the people began to come in for the dance: young men and women and also some older people. At this time the women wore long dresses as was the style. It wasn't long before the dance got going, with the fiddler in one corner of the house and the accordion player in another corner.

The first dance was called the lancers, and although I was a stranger I couldn't keep from enjoying myself. The stranger is always made welcome in Newfoundland. The dance went on until daylight, with short breaks in between. This was to pass around the homebrew and scattered nips of moonshine. Then some songs were sung, and one of the songs that seemed very popular was the "The Star of Logy Bay," a version of which I had written. It was played on the fiddle and the accordion and sung by a young man and a young lady. It made me feel sad and also glad when I thought of my many friends and my people down east and also my childhood sweetheart. The song I wrote went like this:

THE STAR OF LOGY BAY

Ladies and you gentlemen
I pray you will draw near
I will explain the praises
Of a lovely charmer fair
The curling of her golden locks
She had stole my heart away

She was born and her place of residence
Is down near Logy Bay.

I will explain and make it plain
There's a place you all know well
In Torbay, near Outer Cove
That's where my love did dwell
She's the sweetest girl in all the world
So everybody says
May the powers up above
Send down their love
On the Star of Logy Bay.

Her golden hair in ringlets rare
Over her shoulders did entwine
With deep blue, smiling Irish eyes
Her face was fair and kind
I courted her but did not think
Our love would end this way
And I would part
With a broken heart
From the Star of Logy Bay.

Diana was a virgin fair
She was blessed and comely too
But not one kind consentment
Of a woman's word she knew
Now Venus was no fairer
Nor the lovely flowers in May
May God above protect my love
The Star of Logy Bay.

It was on a summer's evening
By the Quidi Vidi side
I asked her in a friendly way
If she would be my bride
"Kind sir," she said, "I am afraid
My daddy he won't okay
He will us part
This will break my heart,"
Said the Star of Logy Bay.

It was on the very same evening
I was walking back that way
I met her scolding father
And this to me did say,
"If you will court my daughter
I will send her far away
She never will return again
While you're in Logy Bay."

I said, "Kind sir, be easy
There's no cause for alarm
I love your daughter Mary Ann
And I don't mean no harm
Please, kind sir, you will agree
Don't send her away
It would break my heart
If I should part
With the Star of Logy Bay."

Early the next morning
He went to St. John's town
Engaged for her a passage

On a ship then outward bound
He robbed me of my heart's delight
And sent her far away
And now I will go a searching
For the Star of Logy Bay.
I first set sail from St. John's town
Across the big blue sea
I prayed that I may find her
Wherever she may be
I searched in vain
Through France and Spain
All the states of the U.S.A.
Nowhere in sight
Was my heart's delight
The Star of Logy Bay.

When I thought the search was finished
Then back in Chelsea, Mass.,
I met a girl there on the street
I watched to see her pass
A great surprise
Was before my eyes
On this fine summer day
For standing there with her golden hair
Was the Star of Logy Bay.

And now, me boys
We are married
As you will plainly see
I love her very dearly
And I know that she loves me
Here's ado to her scolding father

Away from him we'll stay
And we never will return again
While he's in Logy Bay.

I enjoyed the dance very much, and I was really glad that I had made the trip to Millertown. But my stay with my newfound friends was short, for I had to get back to my ship in Corner Brook the next day. When I got on board the train that afternoon, I took along with me happy memories: the logging town, the hospitality that I received, and all the people who treated me, a stranger, so well. We went back once again over the Gaff Topsails and this was a clear fall day. You could view the scenery very plainly.

Most of our passengers were lumberjacks. They all seemed to be whooping it up, singing songs, and playing music, and the smoke was so thick you couldn't see through the train. But everyone seemed to be having a gay time. Sometimes on the Overland Express it got pretty rough, and this day was no exception. Some fights started now and then, but the conductors seemed to be able to keep order among the men.

When everything seemed to be under control, one lumberjack drove his fist through a glass in the door. The glass was smashed to pieces, and the poor fellow, who was awfully drunk, got his arm cut up badly. Blood was flowing from his arm and this caused alarm among the passengers. The conductor was not long in getting the blood stopped by putting a piece of cord around the man's arm and then using a piece of stick that the lumberjacks called a twister. This stick, by twisting it around, tightened the cord around the arm. After a few minutes a doctor came tearing through the train; this doctor was one of the passengers. He bandaged up the man's arm, and the injured man would be taken off in Corner Brook. This accident did not seem to hamper the merrymaking and it still went on. It seems a good time was had by all the lumberjacks and also some of their female companions. I guess this was the custom when the boys and girls got together on the train.

As I was wearing my quartermaster's uniform, one of the lumber-jacks thought I was a captain. Then one of the boys said to me, "What ship do you belong to, captain?" To his question I just smiled and said, "I'm not a captain."

Then he told me, "I have thrown more salt water off my southwester than ever you sailed over."

"Young man," I said, "probably you did, but you must have thrown a lot of salt water off your southwester, and I think I have turned more capes than you have turned corners." This brought a roar of laughter from all the passengers, and my accusing lumberjack seemed to be sorry for speaking. He then turned red and walked down through the car. This ended our little talk.

CHAPTER 7

On getting back on board my ship I learned that the party which went up the Humber River had already returned. They all seemed to be much excited about the sights they had seen. As an American lady put it, "The scenery and the beauty of the Humber River are out of this world. The splendour of the valley is outstanding."

Although I hadn't gone up the Humber River at this time, I was overjoyed to hear the compliments that were paid to the place by the daughter of an American multi-millionaire. It would be a big boost for the Newfoundland Tourism Department if they knew the praise that had been given the area.

Earlier in this story I gave an account of the visit to Port aux Basques and Channel, Newfoundland, but I forgot to tell of our exciting trip to Bay d'Espoir, which is located on Newfoundland's south coast, some 150 miles east of Port aux Basques. At the bottom of Bay d'Espoir is Conne River. So, while the *Whirlwind* was at anchor, we went on a motor launch trip up this river to visit the Micmac Indian tribe. These Micmacs are known to be fine people, and there are many of them on the west coast of Newfoundland.

The trip began early the next morning. We started out at 6:30 a.m. with just enough of the early morning light to guide the motor launch and to see the river banks on each side of the boat. It was a beautiful morning and all eight people aboard were in a gay mood. We were towing one of our dories as was the custom when many landings were to be made along the shore, for the dory could go ashore where the motor launch could not. I was the skipper of the dory, as I had been in many of the places we landed in other parts of the world.

We went up the river and on our way we stopped at several places. Each place was most interesting to me—the log piles after the winter's logging, the babbling mountain streams, and the cedar and birch. We talked to some fishermen who were hauling their smelt nets. From them we got some fresh smelts to bring back on board the ship. We then continued up the river. The Micmac Indians we met received us very coolly, and I was later to find out they did not associate much with white people. They just wanted to be left to tend to their own business. But we bought some of the wares, like woollen socks, mitts, blankets, and also hooked rugs. The ones we did business with spoke good English but preferred their own language. One of our party was an American Crowfoot Indian. He spoke to them in the Crowfoot Indian tongue. As he spoke three or four American Indian languages, he tried them with each one, but they understood none of them. Then one of the Micmac said to Jimmy, our Crowfoot Indian, "What in the hell are you trying to say anyhow? Can't you talk English?"

Our party made arrangements to have their lunch on shore. I was told that we would stay here until late in the evening. On hearing of this, I decided to go back down the river a piece in the dory. As I rowed down the river about half a mile, I noticed a house and barn set back from the riverbank. There was a small dock for a landing and I tied up my boat and walked up to the cottage. I figured that white people must live here. My idea was to ask for a drink of water and to obtain some information concerning the fishing and hunting on the river. But I was not expecting to get the information that I did.

I knocked at the door of the cottage and it was quickly opened by a jolly little white-haired woman, who said, "Good day, sir. What can I do for you?"

"Madam, I would like to get to drink of spring water." She invited me in the house and bade me to sit down on one of the two chairs, near a long table. This table caught my eye, for it ran the whole length of the kitchen, and I wondered to myself what she had such a long table for. She gave me a drink of water, which was really appreciated, for the afternoon was quite warm. Then she began talking to me and asked me what I was doing up here, and where I came from. I told her that I was from the United States. "Oh, my!" she exclaimed. "Did you come from the United States in a dory?"

I smiled and said, "No, madam, I am from a ship which is down in Bay d'Espoir, and I am up this river with a party who are at the Indian village."

"Well," she said, "I don't think they will be very welcome up there, for these Indians don't like to be bothered by white people. They seldom have anything to do with white people themselves."

Our conversation was beginning to get interesting, and I asked, "Madam, are you living here all alone?"

"No, sir," she replied. "I have my husband with me. At the present time he is out hauling his smelt nets."

"Don't you get lonesome here by yourself in this wooded area?"

"Oh, no, sir," she replied. "I have my work to do and that keeps me company."

My next question to her gave me the biggest surprise that ever I got in my life. "Madam, do you have any children?"

"Oh, yes, sir," she nodded. "I have 21 big saucy boys."

"Madam," I said, "you must be joking!"

"No, sir," she said, "I am not joking, and believe it or not, sir, I always wanted a girl." I could see now that this was the reason for the long table. And I asked her where the boys were now. "Well," she said, "they are scattered all over. Some are down on the Labrador, more on the mainland, and they are all away for the summertime. They are all skippers and mates on boats. They go to sea and fish and they all return home for Christmas, so we have 23 at the table for Christmas dinner. When they come back, we have a real family reunion. They bring whisky, beer, and wine with them."

I inquired, "Madam, aren't some of them married?"

"No, sir," she said, "they are all bachelors, and they are all 6 feet tall."

"Who do they take after? Their father?"

To this she smiled and said, "Their father is only a small man, not much taller than me." She was not much more than 5 feet tall. I thanked the lady for the water and her kindness and went back to the dory.

I rowed back to my party and I found them already in the launch and ready for the voyage down the river. After making fast my dory, I got on board myself. Everyone was glad to see me, as they thought I was lost somewhere down the river. I told them the story of my visit to the old lady's cottage. When they heard my story of her 21 sons, they first did not believe it, but when I assured them that this was true, they all seemed anxious and said they would love to pay a visit. I think they would have visited her, but time was getting short and we wanted to get down the river to our ship before dark.

When we reached the ship, everyone was tired, so all went to their rooms for a good night's rest.

We sailed from Corner Brook the next morning, and on our way down the Straits we crossed the Bay of Islands. It was not known to the crew members where we were going next.

It was a long cruise down past Flower's Cove. Then I finally found out from the first mate, Mr. O'Brien, that we were going around Cape Norman to the Straits of Belle Isle. These straits were first navigated by the famous Jacques Cartier in the 1500s. It's a mystery to me why the straits were not given his name, like Magellan who first navigated the waters which bear his name, the Straits of Magellan.

After rounding Cape Norman, we went to Cook's Harbour, where we stayed for two days. There were many interesting places around the shore, where our party took pictures of the flakes and the stages. We talked to many interesting people and were shown around the different places. This is a wide open bay and there isn't much shelter from the rough seas of the Atlantic.

After leaving Cook's Harbour, we continued our cruise and sailed around Cape Bauld, and headed south on the east coast, passing Englee and Fleur de Lys, keeping as close to the coast as possible. This was so we could take pictures of the rugged shoreline, where numerous seagulls and other sea fowl were to be seen. The sights were most interesting to all on board.

We steamed up into Notre Dame Bay to Leading Tickles. Here I had a good chance to view this place, as I had heard so much about it in my boyhood. Many schooners sailed from here to St. John's, and I sometimes watched them from my front porch go past Torbay. Many of these schooners are still in use going to Labrador, up and down the coast in the lumber trade, fishing, and many other activities. Most of them at this time were powered by gasoline engines but still carried full sail.

After leaving Notre Dame Bay, we steamed on down the coast. It was a long run this time down to the Funk Islands. We made a landing on the Funks, using two dories, with two different parties on board. I was with one party and I had a good look at the historic Funks that I had heard and read so much about. The seal hunters told some thrilling stories of this place, mostly about the seal hunt.

The place was very rough, and piles of stone could be seen all over. It was lonely and flocks of seabirds encircled them from many directions. Some fishermen's boats could be seen going in and out, and more of them were catching codfish and other species of fish. As I sat in the dory and viewed this place, my thoughts went back to a story that I had heard when I was growing up.

According to the story, hunters used to visit the Funks in search of seals. On one occasion 25 men were put on the island around the last of November, before navigation closed. They had plenty of supplies and a cook with them. They had to stay there for the winter and wait until the ice floes brought down the seals. They would then get all the seals they could and ice them to keep until navigation opened in the spring.

When the seals began to come in the early part of March, the men used to go out from the island and bring the seals back to land. All 24 of them used to leave the island in the morning and travel to the east, sometimes going 8 or 10 miles, just leaving the cook on shore. One morning as usual they went on their daily tour for seals. While they were gone, a windstorm came up over the ice and the men got trapped on it. The cook on shore could see the poor men when they came to the end of the ice floes toward the island. But the cook was helpless to offer them any assistance. He could not launch a small boat because the wind was so powerful that he would be lost himself. The 24 men were doomed: nothing could be done for them.

As the story goes, the cook put in a lonely time by himself on this rough piece of rocky island on the coast of Newfoundland. He spent two months alone on the island. I think that this man had a true enduring courage. He was not short of supplies, but he was bothered by apprehensions. Sometimes he would wake up thinking he had seen the ghosts of his fellow seal hunters. He said that there was a large seabird which used to perch near the camp every night and its screams could be heard all through the darkness. There were many storms and severe frosty weather while he was there. He was finally rescued when navigation opened in the late spring. He was a total wreck.

After we made several visits to this little rugged island, we steamed up to Cape Bonavista. We took pictures and also made a painting of Cape Bonavista. We tried to land in this area where Cabot, according to the unconfirmed accounts of our Newfoundland historian, had landed. Cabot's name was supposed to be on a rock in this area. I don't think that a seaman like John Cabot would fool around in this rough place off the Newfoundland coast, for surely it would not offer his ship any protection. However, our historians say that he sheltered here to protect his ship. I paid a visit to our museum in St. John's, and as you go in through the hallway, there's a painting. It shows Cabot's ship the *Matthew*, with full sail running on the east coast of Newfoundland. Cabot is standing on the deck with a spyglass, looking at the coastline ahead of him. This picture, if viewed by a farmer, or someone who had never set foot on a ship, might seem all right. But any seaman, especially from Newfoundland, would plainly see two blunders in it. I've never had in all my life an experience wherein we had clear weather with the wind east, on the east coast of Newfoundland.

Now this ship was running from the east to the west with full sail; in other words, running on the land on the Newfoundland east coast, with the sails all blowing full with the wind, the land in full view, and the weather clear. The truth is that it's always foggy with an east wind. There is another big blunder on the part of the artist: Cabot with a spyglass viewing the shoreline in a thick fog. I am told that this artist got $5,000 from the Newfoundland government for his painting.

We crossed Trinity Bay and called at Bay de Verde. We dropped anchor and sent a boat ashore. This was to find out some information on the fishery, as one of our people on board was writing an article on the fishing industry of Newfoundland. We stayed here for five hours; by this time the boat had returned and the *Whirlwind* weighed anchor and resumed her cruise along the coast to Baccalieu.

On reaching Baccalieu, we made three landings in three different places, taking pictures of the cliffs and rugged rocks. From the deck of the ship our artist made paintings of the rugged cliffs of these famous towering heights. There seemed to be thousands of seabirds flying over the high cliffs and perching on the ledges and rough spurs that were protruding from the rocks, on the face of the cliff. All the surroundings were in an uproar of screaming seagulls, herring gulls, murres, man-of-war birds, gannets, and many more.

I was glad when we got away from the shores of Baccalieu and once again headed southward along the coast. At the time we did not know where we were going next; as far as the crew were concerned, it was anyone's guess. Word got out that we were going to St. John's. The thoughts of this made me very happy and I figured I would be able to see my sweetheart, who lived only 7 miles from St. John's in Torbay. I even thought of getting married, if Kay would be willing, for I knew by this time that I loved her very much.

The good ship sailed along the coast on her way to the capital city of St. John's, Newfoundland. Mr. Boland sent for me to report to his quarters on the promenade deck. By this time we were crossing Pouch Cove. This place is located a short distance south of Cape St. Francis, in Conception Bay. When I went up to his sitting room, he greeted me warmly in his usual way. And he said, "Jack, remember you told me during the early part of our trip that you thought John Cabot first sighted Newfoundland in this vicinity near Torbay? As we are getting very close to the area, I would like to look it over and see for myself and also my party where you think the landing was made. As you were born here, you should know the coastline quite well."

"Yes, sir," I said. "I am very familiar with the surroundings."

"Well, then," he went on, "will you go on the bridge and pilot the ship as close to the shoreline as possible? This will give all on board a good view of the principal places that you will point out to us. For I think this will be very interesting to all. I would like to see the man's head in the cliff; as I remember, you called it Cabot's Head."

"Yes, sir," I nodded. "I don't think we will have any difficulty in doing this." So I went on the bridge with the captain and we cruised into Flat Rock Bay.

We came into what we call Seal Cove, Flat Rock. Here there is an iron ladder that goes up over a cliff. The dory was hoisted overboard and I rowed a party of six ashore: Mr. Boland and his two daughters, and a doctor and his wife. We landed on a rough shingled beach in Seal Cove. After the landing the people were looking at the ladder that went up over the steep cliff. Then Jenny, the youngest daughter, started to climb the ladder. She went up about 25 rungs, but then she came back down.

Several of them tried it and went up so far, but it was too much for them to climb the steep ladder. I don't know for sure how many rungs are in this ladder, but I think it's around 150. Then to the surprise of us all, the doctor's wife, who had been looking on all the while, stepped on the ladder and started to climb. Well, as the saying goes, "Like a sailor, up she went." She didn't look down once in her climb but went on up to the top and over. The doctor was awfully worried about his wife, thinking that in her attempt to come down something might happen to her. All eyes were on the top of the cliff and ladder, but there was no sign of the lady on top of the cliff. She was just looking around up there and was in no hurry in coming to the top of the ladder again.

When she finally did appear and looked down, Dr. Brennan, her husband, warned her to stay up there and we would go around from Flat Rock and pick her up. But the brave lady paid no heed to his warning and, to the amazement of all of us down on the beach, she got on the ladder again and started to descend. With the greatest of ease she came down back-first, and landed on the beach. The doctor was so overjoyed when she made the safe landing he put his arms around her and hugged her like a bear! Mrs. Brennan did not seem to think it was anything at all that she had done. She smiled and said, "It's just good exercise!"

After taking many different rocks from the shingled beach as souvenirs, we made ready to shove off again. On getting aboard the ship, again we cruised in around Red Head. According to Granny Dawson, and her account of John Cabot landing at Flat Rock, this was the land that the man in the crow's nest on Cabot's ship, the *Matthew*, sighted the morning of June 24, 1497.

We cruised along by Red Head and came to anchor off the Flat Rock River. We were now where the *Matthew* had anchored on Cabot's landing at Flat Rock. This little fishing settlement is most outstanding. The sea to the east of it, and to the southeast, holds the best fishing grounds on the east coast of Newfoundland. The fish come in here in abundance, mostly with the capelin run, called by fishermen the "capelin scull." It has no pebbled beaches; all around its western waterfront is flat brown stone. At this time many boats were pulled up on this flat barrier; many more fishing boats lay at anchor in the harbour.

Everyone on board the *Whirlwind* seemed very impressed with the scenery at Flat Rock. For this is how the place got its name: the flat red rocks. Each one with a party on board, our two dories landed near a rugged-looking cliff by the river. The other boat went farther to the south and landed on the flat red stone. We all alighted and strolled up the rocks. Here I was surprised to see a gigantic pile of large beach stones, all piled up on top of one another, forming a long wall. Why I was surprised was because this was the kind of wall Granny Dawson described in her story of the landing of Cabot and his crew.

She told me that behind a wall of beach boulders the Beothuk Indians stood and watched Cabot's men walk up from their landing boat. When the men got midway up the flats, the Indians sent out six or seven big Newfoundland dogs to meet them. Cabot's men were frightened, for they thought that these big black dogs were bears. They all started to run back again to their boats, but the Beothuks came out from behind the pile of boulders and made motions to them to stop and in signs assured them that the dogs would not harm them. The white men found out that these dogs were very gentle, as were their masters, who greeted the first invaders in a most friendly way. It was here in front of this pile of boulders the first powwow on the island of Newfoundland took place between the Beothuks and the men from the *Matthew*.

Both our parties did quite a lot of scouting around in the village of Flat Rock. Sheep and goats were in abundance, both in the settlement and along the cliffs. Some of our people from the ship followed the sheep trails along the cliffs on the north side of Flat Rock Harbour and went on up to the top of Red Head. Here was to be found plenty of partridgeberries, and the view from this height was really wonderful—the blue Atlantic Ocean, the seas rolling over the beamer land, and one could see about 10 miles on a clear day! The picking of partridgeberries was really something new for the people from the ship. They picked over 5 gallons of berries and brought them back to the dories. They enjoyed themselves very much and had a lot to talk about when they got back on board the ship.

With everyone on board again, and after a good night's rest, we weighed anchor the next morning. We headed down along by Red Head, where we all had a look at the shape of a woman in the cliff. The old folks referred to her as Cabot's guiding angel, for they claimed that she guided Cabot to his new-found land, as he called it, "Terra Nova."

After leaving Red Head, we sailed around the beamer, which is a long point of rock reaching out into the North Atlantic. There is a lot of shallow water near its point. It is a good place for cod fishing and it's called New Ground. Then we headed west to Torbay. We were now on our way to a very high grey cliff which is sometimes called the Brandies. Up in this cliff, about 40 feet from the top there is a perfect shape of a man's head. It looks like the neck and head, and this was called Cabot's Head. Many people have come from different places to view it. This head was really formed by nature, as there was no way that anyone could reach this part of the cliff. It still stands today for anyone to see. After taking some pictures and having satisfied ourselves with the head in the cliff, the *Whirlwind* headed south, this time on her way to St. John's.

While coming into the harbour of Torbay, my thoughts went back to when I watched the ships go by this same place. I never dreamed in those days that I would be watching the harbour from the sea, on board a ship that was completing a trip around the world. My dream of high adventure had turned to reality.

We were now in the place John Cabot made his observations on the east coast of Newfoundland, according to Granny Dawson's logbook, which she claimed was over 400 years old. It was now all beginning to make sense, bearing out her stories of Cabot's landing by the river, on the rocks of Flat Rock Harbour.

I mentioned earlier the stone foot that I had unearthed on the north side of Torbay, near the place called Treasure Cove, with Cabot's name cut in this stone as well as the name of the discovery ship, the *Matthew*, and the date very clearly outlined—June 24, 1497—and the letters W and E. Now I have come to the conclusion that the letter W indicated that the wind was west, and the E indicated that they were on the east coast of Newfoundland. Now with the wind west on June 24, 1497, this accounts for the landing at Flat Rock. As the *Matthew* was a square-rigged vessel, she could not get into Torbay Harbour against a west wind, but she could easily go across the wind, and this took her to Red Head, where she anchored. From there her small boat, at that time called a jolly boat, was used to visit Torbay Harbour, where the stone foot was buried, to establish claim of the new land for England and His Majesty, King Henry. The British flag is shown on the stone foot, and the foot itself looks like a monk's sandal.

All of this now makes good sense, for if a flag was mounted on the land it would not stay "put" very long before it would be destroyed either by the wind or by other means. It also bears out the question of where the stone first came from. The brown stone is not native to Torbay, but it is native to Flat Rock—from the red cliffs of Flat Rock, Torbay North. It was from the *Matthew*, anchored near Red Head, that Cabot's men made the passage in the ship's small boat to Torbay west beach. This small boat had a mast, a square sail, a jib, and six oars for rowing.

From Torbay, they then went to Outer Cove beach. This beach is located on the far south side of Torbay. At the time of their landing on the beach, June 26, the capelin were rolling in on the sandy beach by the millions. Cabot's men had never seen this kind of fish before and did not know the name of them. One of the men, whose surname was O'Driscoll, picked up a fish and said to his companion, "We will give them a name." Looking down at the point of land, known today as Torbay Point, he called it a cape, and so the fish were called cape-land fish.

On arriving back to the *Matthew*, the sailors were warmly greeted by the crew. At this time of the year on nearly all sand and pebbled beaches could be found tons of capelin rolling ashore. Behind them in the ocean, codfish, haddock, and many other species of fish were in abundance. All parts of Europe were greatly in need of this valuable source of protein.

On June 27, a storm came up and the *Matthew* had to weigh anchor and put out to sea in deep water. Here she rode out the storm. When she returned to land, she anchored near the Brandies. This is the name of the place at the present time, and it is located on the north shore of Torbay. The water is quite deep here and has good holding ground for anchoring.

On the morning of June 28, the small boat left the ship again. This time she made a passage across the bay, crossing the fishing bank now known as Tanton Shoals, and around the point of land later known as Torbay Point. It's about 11 miles to the north of St. John's, Newfoundland. The boat made the journey by rowing and sailing. They reached the Narrows of St. John's at 11 a.m. on June 29, 1497. According to the old logbook, this was the first boat of any foreign nation to enter the harbour of the oldest city on the continent of North America. Although historians claim that the *Matthew* sailed into the harbour, the captain was a very safe commander and would not take any risks going into a place like St. John's at this time. For it would not be safe for his ship. He was not on board the small boat himself at this time. The man in charge of the crew was Dan O'Driscoll. The names of the other seven men are unknown, for the old lady did not give their names in her account of John Cabot's landing. However, she did say they rode into St. John's Harbour, landing on what is known today as the Outer Battery.

After mooring the boat to the shore, they climbed up on the round hill overlooking the harbour. And while they were looking down on the harbour, they gave St. John's its first name: Narrow Passage. This blots out what our historians say about the way in which St. John's got her name. It seems that our Newfoundland history was written with a lot of guesswork. This makes it very confusing for our schoolchildren to read and understand. It also seems that each new edition of our history is different.

It is claimed that St. John's got its name because it was discovered on St. John's Day, June 24. But it really was on June 29, which is St. Peter's and Paul's Day. So why not call it Peter and Paul or either one of the names alone?

Looking down from the hill, the men encountered a strange sight. The entire surroundings were heavily wooded, especially on the north side. But on the south side, which is now known as the Southside Hills, there was more brush and scrub growth. The smoke from the Beothuks' campfires could be seen in many places. The men looking down at this scene did not feel that it was safe to go down and make contact. But after coming down from the hills they were confronted with many Beothuks, who had already come along the shore to where the boat was moored. It was difficult for Cabot's men to understand their sign language, but they knew it was friendly.

This gathering on the Outer Battery, by all accounts, was the first of its kind to be held between Beothuks and white men in St. John's. The Beothuks presented many gifts to their newfound friends. The gifts consisted of animal skins of different kinds and harpoons carved out of bone.

As the boat was rowed away from the Outer Battery, all the Beothuks joined in to chant some kind of song as a token of farewell to their white friends. This shows that the Beothuk Indians were a friendly people in the beginning of our history; it was the white man who in later years caused the trouble that led these true-born natives to disband and scatter.

Cabot's men made their passage back to the *Matthew* and brought with them cheerful tidings of what they had seen in the harbour of St. John's and of their meeting with the friendly Indians. The gifts they had brought back with them were received by Cabot and his men with appreciation.

On June 30, the *Matthew* weighed anchor at the Brandies and sailed north along the coast to continue the investigation of the east coast of Newfoundland. Despite the explorations, Cabot could not tell when he got back to England if Newfoundland was an island or part of a land mass.

As the *Whirlwind* steamed along, I was in high spirits, for the shores of Torbay could be plainly seen, even the movements of the people on the shoreline. We were only about 11 miles from St. John's by sea, and I would soon be home with my parents and many friends and also my childhood sweetheart, Kay. This would be a great surprise to them all in

Torbay. For although they might be watching the ship from the shore, there was no way for them to know that I was on board.

We steamed along, now keeping farther to the east to clear the shallow water of the fishing banks that are located on the south side of the entrance to Torbay. This fishing bank is called the Tanton Shoal. The ship was brought to a stop and handlines were put overboard to try for fish. We were very successful, for codfish were here in abundance. About a hundred big fish were hauled on board the *Whirlwind* and when the party was satisfied that they had enough, we continued on course toward St. John's.

As I was very familiar with the coastline in this vicinity, many questions were put to me in regard to the names of the high hills. One of the hills was outstanding; it was called Sugar Loaf. It was put on canvas by a famous artist, and many pictures were taken of this rugged coastline.

We steamed slowly along in the ship's lane until we cleared the highland beyond Sugar Loaf. Then the *Whirlwind* was put on a course up to the Narrows of St. John's. It was very interesting to view the high cliffs where Cabot Tower now stands. The flags on Cabot Tower could be seen quite plainly as they waved in the breeze, indicating to the people in St. John's that a ship was approaching the Narrows.

On reaching the pilot boat, the *Whirlwind* came to a stop in order to take the pilot on board. After the pilot went on the bridge, we started to steam slowly ahead. We were almost at the entrance to the Narrows when the *Whirlwind* started to turn around. After turning around, she headed out to the open sea. This came as a surprise to all on board and a big disappointment to me. About 10 minutes later she dropped off the pilot. After the pilot boat left the sea ladder, the *Whirlwind* began to pick up on an easterly course. The land astern of us began to fade in the distance.

What had happened was that Mr. Boland, the owner of the *Whirlwind*, had received a message from New York that some of his relations were coming over from Europe on the ocean liner, the *Majestic*. He had to be back in New York to meet the ship. The thought of not seeing my sweetheart made me heartsick for quite a while after.

We steamed past Cape Spear, then on to Cape Race. After passing this famous southern point of Newfoundland, we shaped our course for the *Nantucket* lightship, which was about 1,000 miles away. This was a long run for the *Whirlwind*. The weather was fine, and the task of putting the *Whirlwind* in shipshape order began. Painting had to be done and the decks all holystoned, and we did our best to have the ship looking her finest when she arrived in New York. The yacht seemed to be running at top speed, which was 14 knots, or approximately 15 miles per hour.

CHAPTER 8

On reaching New York, we were just in time to meet the *Majestic*. We went to Brooklyn and tied up in Erie Basin, where we waited for the party that had come over on the *Majestic*. The party arrived about 2 p.m. There were two young women who were Mr. Boland's nieces and also a doctor and his wife, plus a butler and a maid. As I was stationed on the gangplank with another quartermaster, we helped our party up with their luggage. Each one of the newcomers gave us each a $2 bill for a tip.

After the party was on board and settled away in their quarters, the *Whirlwind* cast off lines again and headed out of Erie Basin. This time we were on a trip up the Hudson River. We could see all the skyscrapers on Manhattan Island, along by Bowling Green, with the Statue of Liberty in full view. Some people could be born in New York and never get the chance to view this lofty statue. It must be inspiring for immigrants when they are viewing New York for the first time. Yes, there is something about the Statue of Liberty and what she stands for—freedom and liberty for all.

The *Whirlwind* continued up the Hudson River and up to Bear Mountain Park. Here we stayed for two days. We had shore leave, with plenty of time to enjoy the park, and to inhale some of the good mountain air.

After leaving the park, we steamed back down the coast to Atlantic City. Here we stayed for two more days, visiting the bathing beaches, which by this time were closing down for the season. Our time was beginning to get short. After making two or three more sightseeing trips we headed back to Marine Basin. We were now into late November. After tying up to the dock, we were all notified that the *Whirlwind* was tying up for the winter. The was the end of the voyage of the good ship *Whirlwind*, after making 87 ports in 18 months, which took her around the world and the seven seas. The crew was paid off and Mr. Boland, true to his promise, gave me $800 extra for my weather forecasting on that trip.

Now that we were to go on shore we had to look for more jobs. I felt sad when I walked up the dock in the Marine Basin. Looking back I could see our gallant ship at the dock. I thought of the storms she had brought us safely through and it brought tears to my eyes. Parting with your ship is like the parting of a good friend. I was now on shore in Brooklyn. Generally, a sailor does not spend much time on shore before he looks for another ship, for the sea gets in a sailor's blood. But with me it was a little different. I felt as though I would need a little rest after being so long on the sea.

Two days after being discharged from the *Whirlwind*, I got a job in a Brooklyn shipyard. The pay at this time was 36 cents per hour. The work consisted of heating rivets for the riveters to put into the steel plates. The job wasn't bad, but I worked a week at it and thought all the time about going to sea again. So I quit one morning about 10 a.m. and went up to the office and got my pay. Shipyard work wasn't the life for me.

It was a cold morning with the temperature about 28°F. I crossed Third Avenue and on reaching the other side I met a fellow who had been laid off from the shipyard. At this time there were many men out of work. While I was talking to this fellow, we heard someone screaming from the other side of the avenue. I saw a poor elderly woman all dressed in black with a brown shawl around her head. She had started across the avenue and by this time the icy water was halfway up to her knees. She was crying out for someone to help her. None of the people who were passing by seemed to notice the lady or would lend her a helping hand.

I said to my companion, who was wearing long rubber boots, "Go out and help the poor woman." But the answer he gave me was, "The Hell with her." Although I was wearing low-cut shoes, I rushed out to the aid of the helpless lady. Picking her up in my arms, I brought her to the sidewalk. After setting her down, she said, "God bless you, my boy, and bless those who reared you. You have done a noble deed, and you will be rewarded for it." Staring into my eyes, she continued, "You've got a hard road ahead of you in your life. There will be many crosses that you will have to bear, but you will come through it all and my prayers will always be with you." Somewhat bewildered by her words, I asked her if she was all right now, and she said, "I am fine now, thanks to you, my boy." Then with another "God bless you, my boy," she feebly walked toward Fourth Avenue.

I thought I would never see the old lady again, but in the days that followed I was to see her many times in what I would call a vision or something that I can't rightfully explain. But she did appear at the time when my life was in danger and I thought the end was near. And it seemed that her prediction was to come true in my life on the high seas and the many close calls I had.

When I got home to my rooming house, which was run by my Aunt Nell, she had wonderful news for me. My girlfriend, Kay, was in Brooklyn. The only bad thing about it was my aunt couldn't tell me where to locate her. But she said, "There's a Newfoundland dance tonight at Park Slope Hall, and chances are she'll be there with some of her friends."

When the hall opened at eight that night, I was among the first there. As I watched the people come into the dance, I did not have to wait long when in she came, accompanied by two girlfriends who had been living in Brooklyn for some time. But there she was standing there in the entrance with all her golden hair. It didn't take her long to notice me, and she rushed over and threw her arms around my neck. She kissed me two or three times on the cheek, and the tears rolled down her cheeks with joy.

After the disappointment of not getting into St. John's, it seemed now that my luck had changed for the good. We sat down and talked about our folks back home. She had plenty of news for me and I had plenty to tell her. In the days that followed we went to many places of interest in Brooklyn, especially the dances. This was a meeting place for Newfoundlanders; Irish and American also people attended these dances, and sometimes many other nationalities. The music was furnished by two accordions, playing jigs, reels, waltzes, and all Down East music.

Jack Dodd helped an elderly woman to the New York sidewalk.

I enjoyed myself tremendously, but my mind began to wander back to sea. Day after day I visited the shipping offices, the seamen's institutions in New York, and many ships along the waterfront, searching to ship out again. Then one afternoon it happened. It was in a barroom in Brooklyn. Although it was Prohibition, this place still ran its bar. You could get a drink of beer with a very low percentage of alcohol content, and if you were known to the proprietor you could get a drink of some kind of whisky.

While I was having my glass of needle beer, I saw a young man enter. He was a former shipmate of mine whom I had sailed with out of Boston. This was on a beam trawler and he was mate on her. On seeing me, he rushed over and shook my hand, then asked what I was doing.

"I'm not doing anything at the present time. Only searching around for a chance to go to sea."

Then he said, "Well, search no more. You've got a berth." He went on to ask me about two shipmates who had been with me on the *Whirlwind*. He asked me where he could locate them, and I assured him that I could get in touch with them. He then told me what his proposition was. He was going to captain a two-masted vessel and was to take her to the Panama Canal and to San Diego, California, where she would be sold and the crew would be paid back to New York. The salary would be $100 a month. This was big money in those days, as the average wage paid for going to sea was $65. And I knew my former shipmates would be glad to hear the news, as they were also searching for berths to go to sea.

So I shipped with Captain Dwyer to go on a vessel named the *Columbia*. We were to join her at 23rd Street, Brooklyn, on the following morning. After buying me a drink of beer and promising to meet us the next morning on board the *Columbia* with my two former shipmates, Bill McGrath and Richard Delaney, he left the old saloon.

The *Columbia* was a former Gloucester dory vessel. She was built in Essex, Massachusetts, in the late 1800s, and at that time she was about 60 years old. She had fished on the Banks of Newfoundland, Cape St. Mary's, St. Pierre Bank, the Boston Channel, Georges Bank, and all the way south to Tampico Bank.

She had two stout masts—foremast and mainmast. But she still carried the topmast, as seen on the old-time Gloucester vessels. The idea of this was an extra piece of canvas could be carried on both the mainmast and the foremast. These sails are called the gaff topsails. The other sails were a mainsail, a foresail, jumbo, and two jibs. One is called the inner jib; the other the outer jib, sometimes referred to as the flying jib. She also had a jib boom, which was sometimes called the bowsprit.

The work of getting the *Columbia* ready for sea lasted a week. Then provisions were brought on board and three extra men were hired. This made nine of us altogether, including the captain. On the day before we sailed, the mate was coming down the dock and he saw two rats coming up from where the *Columbia* was lying at the dock. Then before he got on board another rat came down the gangplank. He did not say anything about this to us when he came on board, but he told us about it that night in a barroom on Fifth Avenue. There were four or five of the crew there, drinking needle beer, but they only laughed at his story and it all seemed to be forgotten for the time being. I didn't take it so lightly, however, for I remembered the story about the rats saving the seal hunter's life on the *Southern Cross*. I felt that I would quit the next morning.

The subject came up again for discussion and was smoothed over by the mate, who said, "It must be in the liquor you drank last night."

That night I went to see Kay, and we went to the Prospect Theatre on Ninth Street in Brooklyn. Here we viewed a movie, but it seemed that Kay's mind was not on the screen. She kept talking to me and almost pleading with me not to go away on the *Columbia*. She said that I should give up going to sea and get married and settle down in Brooklyn for a short while. Then, she said, we could go back to Newfoundland, which she loved more than any place in the world.

Kay's idea was the right one, but I did not agree with her at this time; although I loved her very much indeed, I seemed to love the sea more. It's a mystery which is hard to explain clearly. It seems the sea gets you in its grasp and holds you firm, especially when you are young. It's not the pleasures that a sailor finds in strange countries. It's not the drinks that he imbibes or the songs and music or the girl in every port. But it's something that gets in your blood and stays there for keeps.

I was to find out too late how right my sweetheart was. It would have been the best thing for the two of us to have gotten married. If only I had had the sense to listen to her good advice, it would have spared me many hardships, misery, dangers, and many frightening experiences in the days that followed.

It was with a heavy heart that night when I accompanied Kay back to her residence in Bay Ridge. Kay seemed to be very sad and when I said something to cheer her up, she'd try to smile though she was near tears. I promised her when I got back from sea, I would stay on shore for the rest of my life. We would get married and enjoy the happiness that young couples look ahead to in future years. As I made this promise to her, it seemed to cheer Kay a great deal. Her tears were replaced by her familiar smile. By the time we arrived at her house, the two of us were in much better spirits.

When I took her by the hand to say goodbye, she cried like a child. She kissed me several times and hugged me tenderly. She said, "God guide you, Jack, and bring you safely back to me, for I love you dearly." Then we wished each other a fond goodbye. When I walked away, I felt very sad and tears were in my eyes.

Now ready for sea, the *Columbia* sailed away from Brooklyn the next afternoon. Although I was sailing on her, I could not get the thoughts of the rats out of my mind!

We had a fair tide and we headed across toward the Statue of Liberty. We also had a fair wind from the northwest. It was a fine, sunny day in early December. A sailor never feels in good spirits when he is leaving the shore, especially a place like the City of New York, with all its gaiety.

As the *Columbia* made her way across the great bay, you could view the tall buildings on Manhattan Island. Our vessel was driven by a

Palmer engine. This enabled her to cross the bay to where we would hoist our sails. The Statue of Liberty was in full view. I wrote some stanzas as I thought of what she stands for—"Freedom and liberty for all."

There is a grand old lady
Who stands in New York Bay.
She watches ships returning
And sees them sail away
She is a symbol of liberty
And for freedom, she does stand,
She's a noble New York lady
The queen of Yankee land.

It's nice to view Miss Liberty
At the head of New York Bay
Where the immigrant is welcome
In the glorious U.S.A.
And it really makes no difference
Your colour or your creed
All are welcome to America
Where you'll find kind friends, indeed.

As the *Columbia* was a full-rigged sailing vessel and she sailed with the wind and tide, we all turned to hoisting sail. All the sails had to be hoisted by hand, and this was hard work. It was heave ho, heave ho, haul, haul!

When all sail was on, the *Columbia* heeled over with the strain of the wind in her sails until her starboard rail was awash in the sea. The wind was from the west about 25 miles, which is called a good sailing breeze. We sailed down by Fort Hamilton, along by Romer Shoal Light and then headed out for the open sea. We then went down through Ambrose Channel to the *Scotland* lightship. From there we went down to *Fire Island* lightship, and from this lightship we shaped our course to the south and along the coast of New Jersey. As we understood at this time, we were going to go down to the Panama Canal.

Our cargo was gasoline in drums to be landed somewhere in the Panama Canal. The wind seemed to freshen up a bit after we left *Fire Island* lightship. The *Columbia* was doing about 12 knots; as the old sailor's slogan goes, "She had a bone in her teeth." Our crew were busy getting all the running gear coiled up and the anchor secured and doing all the work that's required to get the vessel shipshape after leaving port.

I felt quite lonesome on my first night out. The thought of leaving Kay behind was constantly on my mind, and I promised myself over and over again that this would be my last trip to sea. But sometimes promises are made to be broken, and in my case that is what happened.

Now there is always a bit of gaiety on ships after leaving port, and the *Columbia* was no exception. As I went down her forecastle I found that my shipmates were really making merry. They were passing around a bottle of what they called White Mule. This is white alcohol of a high percentage. One fellow was singing a song, and the words went something like this:

Five men sitting on a dead man's chest
Hey, ho, a bottle of rum.

Then another fellow started to sing another ballad:

Outward bound
Out we must go
Hurrah! My bully boys,
Out we're bound.

I did not drink myself, but I really enjoyed the singing and their gaiety cheered me up. Then another of my shipmates sang:

Outward bound to plow the sea
Our drunken captain went on a spree
He came on board and to us did say,
"Now hoist your sails and we'll be on our way."

We hoisted our sails with his command
With a heavy gale we left the land
We had Cape Pine on our lee
And we forced her out in a heavy sea.

Storm clouds now, overcast the skies
Our ship she's sinking and cannot rise
We asked the captain to shorten sail
Or we'd all be lost in the heavy gale.

He cursed aloud and he tore his hair
Saying, "While I am captain there is no fear
While I am the captain you need not fear
I will shoot the first man who ventures near."

Then up spoke one of our gallant men
Saying, "You're only one and of us there's ten
We will reef her down in this heavy blow
If you interfere you will be tied below."

We reefed her down against his will
It eased her now but the sails kept filled
We are heading out for the Cape Shore now
As she throws the white foam from her bow.

Now we're homeward bound with a deep success
Like a joyful seagull she seeks her nest

When I get on shore no more I will sail
With a drunken skipper in a heavy gale.

Our gaiety in the forecastle was cut short by the loud shout of the mate who called, "All hands on deck!"

I was the first to reach the deck and found that we were now into a howling gale of wind. The wind was northwest, which is a very bad wind on this coast. The *Columbia* was running before the gale and the seas were very high, sometimes coming over her and sweeping her deck from forward to aft.

We were caught with all our sails on in a howling twister. The mate was shouting to shorten sail. He ordered me to go aloft on the main mast and Bill McGrath to go up on the foremast to tie up the gaff topsails. Now in a storm like this, it is only the most experienced sailors who are sent aloft to do this kind of job. As I started up the starboard rigging, I found that it was hard to hold on at times. When I reached the crosstrees and above the piece of canvas was going wild, I found that it was all I could master to hold fast and fold the topsail.

There were times when the *Columbia* rolled over and the masts almost touched the sea. I managed to get two lashings around the piece of canvas. After I got it secured, I made my way down the rigging again. And there were times when she nearly threw me off the ratlines.

When I was about 6 or 7 feet from the deck, one of the ratlines broke underneath my feet. I tried to cling to the rigging, but with a sudden roll of the ship I lost my hold on the rigging and went down on the afterdeck. I did not get hurt, but I was badly shaken for a while.

I found out by this time that Bill McGrath, the man who tied up the fore topsail, had come down safely from aloft. The mate was still shouting orders to the crew, and everyone was on the hop on all parts of the vessel. Some were out on the jib-boom tying up the jibs, while men were tying up the mainsail. All sails were taken down except the foresail. This sail was double-reefed and hoisted again.

The *Columbia* was being constantly swept by heavy seas. But now under shortened sail she would be brought to the wind and would have a chance of riding out the storm. The sea was quite rough, and this was where good seamanship was needed. There were six of us to do the work, and all six were experienced seamen. The mate was a fine sailor and had seen a lot of adventures on the sea. He was right there working with his men; all orders were given by him and were carried out by his crew.

Our captain, who had practically no experience in sail, left all of the orders to the mate. As he was a steamboat man, he had spent most of his time on beam trawlers and in the Merchant Marine. In my opinion it was his lack of experience in sail that would cause him to lose his ship.

The *Columbia* was now taking a bad beating in the rough seas, but under a double-reefed foresail she rode the seas much lighter. Once in a while a wave would sweep over her deck, flooding her bulwarks from stem to stern. It was "hold on for dear life," for sometimes men would be swept across the deck from port to starboard.

The steering wheel was "hove down on her" hard to port, while the vessel herself was on the starboard tack. This is generally done when a vessel is hove to in a heavy storm at sea. And in our position, at the present time, on the Jersey coast, it would not be unusual to get into a bad twister. A twister means a wind of 70 to 80 miles an hour, which kicks up a big sea.

This gale of wind held for 48 hours, blowing from 80 to 90 miles an hour. Then it died down to about 20 miles per hour and the sea became smoother. We shook out the roof of the foresail, the mainsail was hoisted, and the mate gave orders to hoist all sails, for this was a good sailing breeze and the *Columbia* was once more put on her course toward Cape Hatteras.

When all the sails were on and all the running gear was coiled up, the *Columbia* seemed to gather headway and once more was running with the wind under full sail. In such a storm, however, both crew and ship took a bad beating. In the *Columbia*'s case there were many planks broken in her bulwarks (the railing of the ship that goes around on port and starboard sides). Fortunately, the damage to our ship could be repaired at sea. We first thought we were lucky with just a broken bulwark, but we were later to find out that the *Columbia* had more damage below. She was leaking badly and we were kept constantly at the pumps to keep her free.

About 4 p.m., as we were running along under full sail, the captain gave orders to the crew to keep the pumps manned and we would be paid $1 extra per hour. The captain, in a case of emergency at sea, represents the insurance company. In order to save the vessel from sinking, the crew had to keep pumping all the time.

The captain now decided on making the first port he could, which was somewhere along the coast of Carolina. As darkness set in, with all our crew pumping, just taking time off to have supper, we seemed to be able to keep the water in the hold at a medium level. But as time wore on, it looked as though we were losing the battle, for the soundings in the hold showed that the water was slowly gaining on us.

The wind had freshened quite a bit and it was now blowing about 45 to 50 miles per hour, with mixed snow and sleet. The crew were busy at the pumps and all held out hopes that we would make port before the night was out. Then there was a clearing in the snow squall, and the man on the bow lookout reported there was a light ahead. This brought both the captain and the mate up to the bow in order to find out what light this was. In my opinion, the captain didn't know what land we were near. However, he didn't get time to tell by the flashes of the light because we saw breakers ahead. We were too close to the breakers to manoeuvre.

With the *Columbia* doing about 12 knots before the wind, she went right upon top of the reef. She struck pretty hard and it seemed that her first contact with the reef had ripped the bottom out of her. The seas were breaking over her in all parts. Everything was in confusion. The mate was hollering to let the sails run. This was done and all the canvas came down on the deck, with the seas pounding into the canvas.

The foremast broke off from the impact of the vessel and went over the starboard side. There was a mass of rigging and canvas over on the opposite side of the vessel. The men were hollering to man the lifeboats.

The first lifeboat was put over on the port side, and three or four men jumped into her, including me. Then a big sea broke over the *Columbia* and down on top of the lifeboat, smashing her to matchwood. What was left of her floated away in the breakers. Out of the four, only two of us survived. The other two fellows were never seen again. How I managed to survive, I can't clearly describe. Both me and the other man were thrown in on the deck. Then we went to get the other lifeboat over but we were stopped by the mate from launching her.

We only had two lifeboats. The mate, who used good judgment, warned us that the same thing would happen to the other lifeboat.

It was due solely to the mate's good judgment and seamanship that any of us survived. The *Columbia* was all broken up on the starboard side. A strip of her deck was already broken down and all of her starboard bow was beaten to pieces. Then the mate gave us the order to get the lifeboat over. When the boat hit the water, six of us got into her. This time we were lucky enough to get away from the side of the vessel. But our boat became half full of water in trying to get away.

There were times when we came near to turning over, but somehow we managed to get clear of the breakers. We then discovered that the mate was still on board the *Columbia*. It was impossible to go back for him. And it looked at first that our brave mate was doomed. Then one of the men saw the mate go aft on the wreck and jump over the stern. It appeared that he had committed suicide, for the seas were mountainous around the wreck.

The captain of the lifeboat told us to row around the wreck. Then he said to row around the reef and over to where the *Columbia* first went on the shoal. As there was a flashlight in the lifeboat, Captain Dwyer was now flashing it toward the wreck. We then spotted the mate in the water, with the breakers going over his head. The brave man was swimming like a Newfoundland dog. We started to bring the lifeboat toward him and we finally got hold of him, but we could not get him on board. The lifeboat was very small, and she had six men on board and was half full of water.

We were still on the edge of the breakers of the reef, with a very rough sea and a 50-mile gale. We put a line around the mate's waist in order to take the strain off his arms, as he was clinging to the stern of the lifeboat. We all leaned over on one side and the mate was finally pulled on board. Other than exhaustion, he was none the worse for his battle with the rough seas.

All the men in the lifeboat were wet. Some of us were poorly clad. I myself had rubber boots, light khaki pants, and a lightweight shirt. But I had an old southwester on my head. I came to have this on was because it was the first thing I put on when I went to put my oil clothes on, and the old southwester was keeping my head dry.

We were still near the reef, and, as the night wasn't terribly dark, with the help of a powerful flashlight we could still see the reef from the lifeboat. We could also see our vessel, what was left of her, where she was held hard and fast, being pounded to pieces by the heavy seas.

We did not have long to watch her. A big wave descended on the *Columbia*, covering her with white foam. We then heard a loud cracking sound from the vessel and she broke in half. The forward part rolled over the eastern end of the reef as if it was a matchbox. Then it disappeared from view into the breakers, as if a monster had swallowed it. A few seconds later, the other half, which was the stern part, disappeared from view. So the once-proud sailing ship *Columbia* was now gone to the graveyard of lost ships.

The captain looked at his watch; it was 9:30 p.m. Then he said, "It's just two hours from the time that we struck the reef and now our ship has broken up and disappeared."

This was my second shipwreck, and it had happened so suddenly it was hard for me to believe that it was true. As I said in the early part of this story, I cried when my first ship, the *Diana*, went down in the North Atlantic. Now my second shipwreck caused me to cry again. I felt so very sad watching her get beaten to pieces that it brought tears to my eyes. For a sailor who loves his ship to watch her go down makes him feel desolate indeed—especially when he is adrift in a small open boat, overloaded with men, as was our boat at this time.

We did not know our position, but we were somewhere off the Carolina coast. The captain could not figure out where the reef was located. As he said, the chart did not show any reef. All we could do now was keep the heavily loaded boat ahead of the wind, in order to keep her from swamping. We were still very close to the breakers, but we were keeping a safe distance from them, with the boat stern still toward them.

Then a very strange and unusual thing happened. The words of the old lady, whom I had rescued in Brooklyn, came back to me: "God bless you, my boy, and keep you away from all dangers. Although you will face many hardships and crosses in your future, you will come through them all, for my prayers will guide you always."

I could not believe my eyes. There, astern of the lifeboat, not far from the reef, was the form of a woman. There seemed to be a bright glow of light all around her. She seemed to be approaching the stern of the boat until I could see her quite plainly. She was the image of the woman in Brooklyn.

I asked the men in the boat to look astern, thinking that they would all be able to see this phenomenon too, but no one except me saw anything. As we rode away, I could still see the vision standing there with her hand upraised as if she were guiding us on our way. A similar vision appeared to me four times afterwards in my life. She always appeared when my life was in peril and I always came through. I came to know her as my guardian angel. However, as this was the first time, I was really puzzled.

We were now rowing away from the cruel scene of the reef, with no idea as to where we were going. But we had to keep the boat headed into the wind and could not let her go side-on at any time. We only had two oars on board, and we were leaking badly. It was all one man could do to keep the water bailed out. Constantly bailing water was a back-breaking job. The weather was very cold, with rain and sleet. It was a night that I will always remember.

One man was very sick. He was our supercargo and he was suffering from a bad case of seasickness, which he had since we left port. Now seasickness is about the worst sickness that anyone can have. Some people going to sea never get cured of it. A seasick sailor is a man who's no good on a ship. But, then, it's not the poor man's fault. The bosun was an Irishman by the name of Paddy O'Driscoll, and he was worried about his little dog left on the vessel.

Everyone began talking about the dog, for it was only now that we thought about him. The dog, asleep in the cabin at the time of the wreck, hadn't been seen, not even on the deck, in all the confusion after we had crashed. The captain said to Paddy, "You are lucky to be here yourself."

The big Irishman, with tears in his eyes, said to the captain, "I will never be able to get another dog like Brownie."

Then Mr. Bruce, the mate, pointed out, "From the way it looks now, you will probably not need a dog." This ended the conversation about the ship's dog, Brownie.

We were paddling along slowly against the wind. I was rowing, along with my shipmate Bill McGrath. Toward midnight the wind seemed to die out a bit, but the rain was much heavier. The water was getting a little smoother, but the chill in the air would cut you to the bone. It was all right for me and McGrath, who were rowing, for this work kept our blood in circulation. We asked several times to be relieved on the oars, but the captain would not allow any changes. He was afraid that changing the men on the oars of the boat would make a difference in the handling of the boat. So he asked us to remain at our posts for as long as we could hold out.

It didn't become daylight until about 7 a.m. By this time we thought we could hear a ship's whistle. The whistle was a little toward our starboard bow. Both the mate and the captain decided we should keep on rowing toward the sound of the whistle. Around 8 a.m., the wind changed to the east, and it became thick with fog. There was still no letup in the cold rain that was falling.

Then we could hear the sound of a bell, which cheered us up a bit.

The bell only sounded at intervals, about every 15 seconds, as the captain timed it with his watch. At first we thought it was a ship anchored, but the captain overruled this and said that it was a bell buoy. We were then ordered to head for the sound of the bell.

After rowing in its direction for about half an hour, the big red-framed buoy was visible. It was rolling up and down and going wild with the wash of the waves. We could not go near it, as it would crash our boat. Our captain knew that this was a channel buoy, and we were in a ship's channel; but what channel it was, we did not know. The captain told us to keep on rowing, as we might find other buoys in the channel. We heard no more sound of bells, but we could still hear the loud howl of a whistle that sounded like a ship's steam whistle.

The sea had become quite calm. The fog was as thick as pea soup, and there was no letup in the rain. We were all like drowned rats in a tub and almost numb with the cold. Then Paddy O'Driscoll, who was in the bow of the boat, announced, "Look! There's land!"

It was land all right, and we had rowed right onto it in the fog. We could all see it now. It was a nice sandy beach but we were not lucky, for, as Paddy put one leg over the boat to step on the sand, he came near to being swallowed up by quicksand. It was lucky for Paddy that he was clinging to the boat, or he would have been pulled into the dreaded quicksand.

We had quite a time trying to get the boat out of the quicksand, but we managed to get her free. We then cruised along the beach, testing the sand with our oars. After several attempts had been made to land on the beach, we finally found a place where the sand was firm. We then made our landing on the big white sandy beach. Up the beach we could see a grove of coconut palms.

We were later to find out that we had come ashore in the place called the Dismal Swamps in North Carolina. The captain and I took a walk up the beach to see if any people were to be found. But on our way up the beach we could make out in the fog a small animal that was running toward us. We were in for an unexpected surprise, for this little animal turned out to be our lost mascot, Paddy O'Driscoll's dog Brownie.

He was jumping all around us and wagging his tail. But he did not tarry long with the captain and me but raced wildly down the beach to where his master was standing near the lifeboat. We were told by some of the men when we got back that, on seeing the dog coming back, Paddy took Brownie up in his arms, hugging him as if he were a lost child who had returned. Meanwhile, tears of joy rolled down his cheeks.

The captain and I went into the coconut grove on the island, following a small, partly grown-over trail which led to a swamp. Here could be seen many alligators and also snakes. We had to abandon our walk along the trail and return to the beach. We then followed the beach around more closely to the water's edge. It took us about an hour to walk all around, for this was only a small island. There were no human beings living on it. So we had landed on an uninhabited island! We looked for drinking water, but there was none to be found, except the water in the swamps. This, we decided, was not fit to drink. We made our way back to the lifeboat and our shipmates. It was now 2 p.m. We all were still in our wet clothing since the night before. We had not eaten or had anything to drink for more than 21 hours.

Around 3 p.m. the fog cleared away; the wind had already changed to the west and we could see a lighthouse about 1 mile across the river. This accounted for the whistle we had heard blowing in the early part of the morning. It was the lighthouse on the mainland, near the entrance to George's River. We were 16 miles from George's Town, as we were later to find out.

So it was all hands aboard the lifeboat for the trip across to the lighthouse. On reaching the other side, we contacted the lighthouse keeper. We were surprised to find that he could not give us anything to eat. Believe it or not, he was short of grub because the supply boat had developed engine trouble up in George's Town a week before. However, she was expected at any time. The keeper supplied us with hot coffee and came with us to the little landing to speak to the captain of a small fishing boat.

The captain of the fishing smack did not carry any provisions other than a lunch for himself and his two men. So we were out of luck again for anything to eat. Our captain asked him if he would take us to George's Town, telling him that we were a shipwrecked crew who were wet and hungry. He did not seem to want to take us at first. But then he said to our captain, "I will take you up for $75."

The captain reminded him that we were a shipwrecked crew and two of the men were sick and badly in need of medical attention. But this did not change the mind of the captain of the fishing smack. His price was $75 in advance, or we could stay where we were. So our captain said to him, "All right, here is your $75."

The captain of the fishing smack took us on board and we made the trip up to George's Town, arriving there at 8 p.m. Captain Dwyer told us to go into the first restaurant we could find while he went to report to the authorities the loss of his ship and what had happened to her. He also went to the police station, where the police gave him two bottles of whisky for his crew. In addition, he got back the money which he had paid the fishing captain for taking his shipwrecked crew to George's Town. Any shipwrecked crew were supposed to be taken without charge.

We went to the first restaurant we could find. We took two tables, as there were six of us. After we were seated we were approached by a waitress, who greeted us in typical Southern style. They were very friendly and presented each table with a menu. We all ordered roast chicken—our first food in about 28 hours. The whisky was more than welcome; each took a belt of it. Our clothing was still wet, and we were in dread of catching pneumonia. It's a mystery to me why some of us didn't get sick from the terrible cold and the rain and sleet of the night before in the lifeboat.

Our good friend Paddy took two big drinks of the whisky—one for good measure, as Paddy put it. He was really overjoyed at having Brownie back, and this now was the conversation around the two tables. He ordered a T-bone steak for Brownie. This seemed peculiar to us, and Bill

McGrath asked Paddy, "Why not give him roast chicken? Any dog that has swum 27 miles is entitled to roast chicken."

"He doesn't like chicken," Paddy explained, so the waitress brought Brownie an order of T-bone steak. This he ate very quickly, for poor little Brownie was really starved. After he finished the steak, the waitress returned from the kitchen with some roast beef. This he finished off with a vanilla ice cream cone. After this, he seemed to be satisfied.

Brownie was classed now as a real hero by his shipmates. But we were all puzzled why we didn't see any sign of him that night around the lifeboat. He had swum pretty well the same course that we had rowed. But according to the lighthouse keeper, the dog had come ashore near the lighthouse. This would be a mile and a half to the north of where we had landed. And he was an hour and a half later in landing than we were. But the brave Boston terrier was again with his shipmates from the ill-fated *Columbia*.

Paddy told us how he first got Brownie. He was on his way home from work one morning, walking across the Boston Commons, when he found this little pup. He stopped and patted the little fellow, who had probably strayed away from his home. He followed Paddy home and Paddy's wife took him in and fed him. From then on they became good friends. He was two years old now, very intelligent and trained to do quite a few tricks.

When Paddy left South Boston to go to New York, the dog followed him to South Station in Boston. When he discovered that the dog had followed him to the station, he did not have time to go back home with him because he would miss his train to New York. So he had to take him on the train and then on the *Columbia*, where he became the mascot of the crew.

The skipper did not eat with us, for he was away somewhere on business. The supercargo, who was very sick, and also the bosun had to get medical treatment. They were moved to a hospital for observation. After we finished our meal, we were sent to a hotel for the night. We did not need anyone to rock us to sleep when we got in bed: we hadn't had any sleep for nearly 35 hours! We did not get any change of clothes, so we still had to travel the next day in our sea clothes. But we were told that we would get fresh clothes when we got to Washington, DC.

The news of going to Washington put quite a stir in our conversation. While we talked, the mate brought up the rats he had seen leaving the *Columbia*. It seemed that he wanted to get back at his shipmates, who told him that it must be in the liquor he was drinking. "Now," said the mate, "you thought I was crazy. But it's been proven down through the years that when the rats leave a ship it's a signal for everyone to leave as well."

As the mate spoke, it brought back to me my other experience regarding rats leaving a ship, the *Diana*, and the story of the old seal hunter on the *Southern Cross*. There is something about these animals that send out a warning which is usually ignored but should be taken quite seriously. We found out that our two sick shipmates had recovered and would be leaving for Washington with us the next afternoon.

We arrived at Union Station on December 18, 1924. It was my first time in Washington. We could see the White House from the station and at 7 a.m. the capital city of Washington seemed to be still sleeping. We stayed in the station for about an hour and then at about 8 a.m. we strolled down the street, all seven of us, with the captain in the lead. We were looking for a restaurant to get our breakfast.

We went into the first "classy" restaurant we saw. But we didn't expect to receive as cold a reception as we got. This was on account of the way we were dressed—with rubber boots and some of us had on old sweaters hauled over our backs. Our beards were long, as we hadn't shaved for more than a week. Some of us had sea caps on and I was wearing my southwester hat.

The headwaiter met us just outside the door. He stopped us and said, "You are not allowed in here in such clothes." He really thought that we were a bunch of bums, coming into a classy restaurant where you could see yourself in a big mirror every way you'd turn.

The captain shoved the headwaiter aside, telling his men to stay where they were and not to go out, as he asked to see the proprietor. It wasn't long before he appeared on the scene. The captain then told him that we had lost our ship on the Carolina coast and were now on our way back to New York. This was the reason we were all wearing shabby clothes.

The proprietor said, "All right, captain, your men will be given anything they want." He took full charge in seating us at the tables and put two waitresses in charge of us. This was the classiest restaurant I was ever in. While we were there many people who were connected with the White House came in, including senators and congressmen. We had Brownie with us and the people did not know what to make of his sitting down wagging his tail and looking up at the table.

One of the waitresses jokingly said to the dog, "And what are you going to have, my little fellow?"

Brownie barked at her twice. Then Paddy said to the waitress, "He wants a T-bone steak with an extra bone."

The waitress laughed and said, "You understand his language!"

With a big smile, the Irishman said to her, "I ought to, for he's lived with me for two years." We all had pork chops and French fries for our breakfast, with toast and coffee. After we finished our breakfast, the captain told the waitress to put it all on the one bill and he would pay for it himself. The waitress said, "All right, sir," and then she walked across the restaurant to where the proprietor had his office. Shortly after she left the table, the proprietor came over to talk to us.

He asked us if we had everything we wanted. The captain assured him that we did and that all of us were grateful for the good treatment. Then the captain said to him, "Would you be so kind as to give me the bill?"

He said, "There is no bill, captain. It is all on the house." He then invited us back to lunch, but the captain told him we were getting the train out of Washington for New York before noon.

CHAPTER 9

After we left the restaurant, we all walked down the street and back to Union Station. It was now 9:30 a.m. and it seemed that Washington had awakened. The whole city was a beehive of activity. On reaching the station, I sent a message to Brooklyn telling my aunt that I would be arriving home the next afternoon. I mentioned in the telegram that we had lost our ship. After this we got the train from Washington and arrived in New York late the following morning.

When I got back to Brooklyn and went home to my rooming house, my aunt was overjoyed to see me, for she had already heard the news. She was going to have a welcome-home party for me that night. Everything had been arranged for the party, and many guests had been invited, including Kay. Although I hadn't been gone long, my aunt was in high spirits to have this social for me.

At about 7 p.m. the guests started to come in and among the early arrivals were Kay and her two friends. She started to cry with joy as she put her arms around my neck. After we were seated in the parlour, she told me that she had dreamed about the *Columbia*. When she told me her dream, I was surprised, for her dream was pretty close to reality. As I mentioned in the early part of this story, this same girl had dreamed about the wreck of the *Diana*. Kay said that she was greatly worried and she thought that we had all been lost. But she was overjoyed when she heard the news from New York that most of the crew had survived and landed safely on the Carolina coast. Then my aunt's telephone call to her told her that I was all right and on my way home from Washington. "Now," she said, "you must keep your promise. No more going to sea. You must stay on shore and we will do as we planned."

"You are right, darling," I nodded. "I've been taught a good lesson, and I will try my best to give up the sea and get work on shore."

I did feel at this time that going to sea was a rough life, and I felt like having a rest. But then again, as I said before, it's hard to get the sea out of one's blood!

The people were coming in for the party; there was wine to drink, refreshments, and the dining room was decorated with flowers. Then a fellow came in with an accordion and the parlour was turned into a dance floor. Our guests were Newfoundlanders and Irish. There were five Irish colleens from the old country who danced jigs and hornpipes for us. Then we had quadrilles, lancers, and waltzes. This lasted until about 1 a.m. I then took Kay home to Bay Ridge.

I really felt happy that night. I was glad to be alive, especially when I thought about what I had gone through on the *Columbia*, the misery of that night in the open boat, and the loss of my two shipmates who were not as lucky as the rest of us.

On leaving Kay that morning, we arranged to meet again that night. I returned to my aunt's residence on President Street in Brooklyn.

Aunt Nell wanted me to marry Kay and live in the same house with her and her husband. They had a big house and she had no children of her own. It looked good to me and for a time I thought I was going to take her advice.

It was while I was at my aunt's house that I wrote two songs of my memories:

THE TOWERING HEIGHTS OF OLD NEWFOUNDLAND

Down memory lane again I am strolling
To view the land of my youth and birth.
And live again my early childhood

Back in the freest land on earth.
With her hills surrounding with valleys bounding,
Her moonlight streams and lakes so grand.
With her coastline splendours that do surrender,
The towering heights of old Newfoundland.

By the mountainside where I first met her
You look so neat in a cotton band
In a thousand years I would not forget her
On the towering heights of old Newfoundland.

Down the mountain path where we skipped together
And by a babbling brook while the lark did sing
We vowed our love would live forever
And would bloom like the roses in early spring.

But roses fade when the blooms are blighted
Petals die without the dew
Like a pretty girl when her heart is slighted
Now I have faded and so have you.

By the garden gate where we kissed and parted,
And last I held your loving hand
When I sailed away I was broken-hearted
On leaving you and old Newfoundland.

Your mountain paths, your mossy valleys
Bring back memories of the days gone by
Your mountain streams, the silvery moonlight
And the lark's sweet song in the clear blue sky.

Now it's twenty years since from you I parted
And sailed away from my native land,
But twenty years on the stormy ocean
Have not changed the scenes on your hills so grand.

I would love to view from the Cabot Tower
Quidi Vidi by the old bandstand
And the Bannerman Park for a pleasant hour,
On the towering heights of old Newfoundland.

If I could turn back history's pages
My childhood to live again,
I would stay and stray in thee of ages
On the towering heights of Newfoundland.

FLAT ROCK HILLS

In my memories again I am strolling along
While the birds in the trees are singing their song,
To the place of my childhood, through its valleys and dales,
I'm just strolling along on the old Flat Rock Hills.

I'm strolling down winegap along by the shore,
To a place on the hillside called Bowring's Grand Store
To the banks of the river wherein the sea spills
I'm just strolling along on the old Flat Rock Hills.

Your old familiar coastline, your valley and stream
To your gay garden parties and the old chapel green,
Where the boys and the girls turn out for their thrills
Oh, it's nice to be back on the old Flat Rock Hills.

Where our fathers and mothers were born and were bred
By the trade of the beamer and dear old Red Head,
Where they smile as they toil, with the art of their skills
And they stayed and they greyed on old Flat Rock Hills.

It's the place of my childhood, my own happy home,
Here I've got friends, away I've got none,
Here I strayed and played in her valleys and hills
In my golden and happy childhood in the old Flat Rock Hills.

To the big river bridge on an evening in June,
To enjoy the village dancing, by the light of the moon,
With the sound of happy laughter and old-time quadrilles,
Is among my happy memories of the old Flat Rock Hills.

The times may have changed but the old bridge still stands
Just the same as when there we stood hand in hand,
With its old stone foundation, supporting its sills,
And the old river she still roars down the old Flat Rock Hills.

Your sons and your daughters have sailed over the sea
In search of employment in the land of the free
In the place called America, there's sunshine and thrill
But their hearts they left behind them on the old Flat Rock Hills.

From you Old Flat Rock Hills, why did we part
Here's a help to your people from the threads of my heart,
And may I live to see again your valleys and dells,
Just to behold and stroll again down the old Flat Rock Hills.

My stay in Brooklyn was an enjoyable one. I got some needed rest and Kay and I saw a lot of each other. But still my mind was not made up to look for work on shore, for the urge of going to sea was still with me. So I looked around for another ship!

One morning I received a letter from the shipping office offering me a job on a ship going to South America. That afternoon I went to see the man who had sent me the letter. He gave me to understand that the ship was a cargo carrier that was doing business freighting from port to port, mostly in South America. But they told me that sometimes she returned to New York. This interested me very much, for the longest I figured we'd be away would be a couple of months. The job was that of quartermaster and the salary was $100 per month.

I decided on taking the quartermaster's berth. He told me that we would not have to sign on until the ship was ready for sea, as she was now under repairs and would not be ready to sail for five or six weeks.

Going back to sea meant breaking my promise to Kay, and I knew very well that she would be against it, but I did not realize at this time that she would take the stand she did. When I met Kay that night, I tried to tell her in the nicest way that I could. "Kay," I began, "I have something to tell you, and I think it's for the good for us both. I know I promised you I would not go to sea again, but, my dearest, I want you to try and understand, for there isn't much else I can do at this time. Jobs are scarce on shore, and I think that anyone who can get a job—even by going to sea—is very lucky. And, as you know, my luck on my last ship caused me not to make any money.

"At the present time I am only spending the little I had saved on the *Whirlwind*. This won't last long, with all going out and nothing coming in. I was lucky to get this job through a friend in the shipping office. They pay good money and I don't think that the ship will be long gone. And when I return I will be in a much better position to get married."

Then Kay spoke, "I suppose promises are made to be broken, but it's not good to make too many promises. I can't agree with having someone who is here today and gone tomorrow. As you know, when a girl is keeping company with someone going to sea, it means a lot of worry and lonely thinking, not going out with anyone else and just trying to be faithful to one who is always going to sea."

The way she spoke and the way she was so filled up, I pitied her and could fully understand the way she felt. She was really against my going. Then she tried again to persuade me to give it up. She said that if I loved her enough I would change my mind. I ended the conversation by saying that I would think it over and perhaps I might give up on the ship. It was still five or six weeks until I had to sign on, and in this time perhaps I could get a job on shore. She told me that I should go back the next day and tell them that I wasn't going. I said that I would, and she then told me in her sweet gentle way, "You don't have to worry about money, for I am working at a good job, and I also have a bit of money put away for a rainy day. We will get along all right. Stay on shore with me."

I then said, "I am grateful to you, but that is something I could never do. Having to depend on a girl for money is not for me, especially when there's a job to be had, even if it means going to sea."

I knew that I had a decision to make, for it was either Kay or go to sea again. And a decision like this is a very difficult one. However, I knew Kay was waiting for an answer. It's hard to give up someone you love but it seemed that now I had no choice. I never thought for a minute that Kay could turn so quickly, as we were very much in love with each other. But I was mistaken, as I was later to find out. Perhaps it was puppy love that we carried on since childhood, but Kay was not the same with me after this.

As time passed by she kept on asking me if I had given up the ship yet, but each time I told her that I hadn't made up my mind yet. Once she said, "I want your answer soon, Jack."

The time had come to sign on the ship. Thinking that Kay might agree, I went ahead and signed on, but I was surprised one night to find out that Kay had gone to a show with a fellow who was working on shore. He had a good job, as I was told by a girlfriend of Kay's. I figured from the beginning that, if Kay wanted this young man, it would be her affair and I should not interfere. So this is what I did, but I found it very difficult.

It was not easy to forget a girl like Kay, after seven years of keeping company with her. But sometimes the best of friends must part, even the fondest true lovers, so I decided to try and forget. But my heartbreak was very severe, and I did not think that time would change the way I felt. I was in hopes that Kay would change her mind about the other fellow and come back to me. But all my hopes were in vain.

Here are two little verses that I wrote at that time:

My roving ways and crazy notion
With it all my love it fell.
And ploughing on the stormy ocean
I lost the girl I loved so well.

If I had taken her advice and planning
From one so sweet, so meek and kind
For she did have the right understanding
That loving childhood sweetheart of mine.

One night I went to a party on 11th Street in Brooklyn. It was a going-away party for an Irish girl who was going home to Ireland. The people who owned the house were Irish, by the name of Smith. It was a gay affair. Most of the girls were Irish colleens who danced jigs and hornpipes to the music, and everyone seemed to be enjoying themselves but me. I thought that if I had a few drinks it might help. Then I decided this would not be the right thing to do. For all my experiences I learned that it was the best policy to keep sober and always to have your right senses.

I was talking to a friend of mine when I saw two girls come in and join the party. One of them was a girlfriend of Kay's. My spirits rose on seeing this girl, for I thought that Kay might be with her. But I was disappointed, for she was not with them.

Kay's friend, Kathleen Collins, came over to talk to me. She was a sweet-looking girl with big blue eyes that complemented her wavy brown hair. To crown her beauty she had a delightful smile. She seemed to be sorry for me, and she did not think that Kay was doing the right thing by giving me up for this other fellow. She gave me to understand that Kay was sorry for what she had done and she would like me to go and see her or call her up. I told Miss Collins that I had no intentions of doing that and if Kay wanted to see me, she knew where to find me. She said that she would tell Kay.

After this we had a dance together and I found that Miss Collins was a very enjoyable person. When the dance was over, I escorted her home, and her company seemed to cheer me up. We met several times after this and I soon learned that Kathleen was quite interested in me. She had a different attitude than Kay in regard to my going to sea. She thought that I was doing the right thing by getting enough money to provide for the future. As for being away for a while, she said, "Absence makes the heart grow fonder."

I began to enjoy Kathleen's company very much. And I think it was her encouragement and cheerful ways that picked me up from the depths of despair. I still had hopes of meeting Kay again, but apparently she would not give in, after all. I did not think that it was my place to apologize. Shortly after this Kay became engaged, and so ended any hopes for me and my childhood sweetheart ever becoming lovers again.

Well, my mind was still bent on going to sea. So one morning I went to 136th Street, New York, where the ship was tied up to the pier. She was quite a big ship in the oil-burner class; in other words, she was a steamship. I never did find out where she was built. She was now all painted and would be ready to sail in about a week. There were quite a few of her crew members working on her, overhauling the lifeboats, and some were painting. Her two cooks were on board, along with some stewards and mess boys.

After seeing the chief mate, I was put to work shining the brass in the pilot house and different pieces of brass on the lower and upper bridge. As I was one of the quartermasters, I worked with two other fellows, who seemed to be two fine friendly chaps, and I felt I would get along with them fine. They were both American. I was later to learn that one fellow came from New York and the other from Brooklyn.

The chief mate also seemed to be a nice man. He kept on chatting as we worked. His name was Mr. Freeman and I think his home was in Maine. I was very curious to know where the ship was going, so I asked the mate what was the ship's destination after she left New York.

"We really don't know where she will be going. When we leave New York, we'll be sailing under sealed orders. So it will be anyone's guess as to our destination."

This was my first time sailing under sealed orders, and I was not really satisfied with the mate's statement.

I ate my first meal on the ship that day, and found the mess hall was up to date and the food was excellent. The two mess boys wore white uniforms and they seemed to be friendly with the crew. After dinner we went back to work again, as there was plenty of brass to shine and it seemed as though she had not had a true shining for years.

We quit work at 5 p.m. and I went back to Brooklyn by way of the subway. When I arrived at my Aunt Nell's house, I found her in a very sad mood. She was disappointed, for all the plans which she had made for me now seemed to be a failure. She had heard the news about Kay's engagement and felt so bad about it that she was going to call Kay up and ask her to come down to see her. I advised her against doing this, as I wanted to let it stand as it was. So I told her that it would not be the right thing to interfere with anyone's private life.

Up to now she had not heard about my going out with Kathleen. Although she knew the girl well, she was surprised when I told her, "If you want to call someone, why not call Kathleen?" This is what she did.

Kathleen came down to the home at 8 p.m. There was always a bit of fun going on at my aunt's house. We had a game of cards and Aunt Nell, who played the accordion, played some Down East music. I took

Kathleen home that night and enjoyed her company, but I still couldn't get Kay out of my mind.

The next morning I went back to the ship as usual, doing the necessary work that had to be done in order to get a ship ready for sea. I liked the ship, but on the other hand it was like something had snapped inside of me. This trip was different from all the other trips. As I said before, my love for the sea was very great all my life. But now it looked like the sea had done something to me, and when I gave it some thought, it really had. For it was through the sea that I had lost the girl I loved.

Our stay in port was now getting short and the ship was almost ready for sea. They began taking on the cargo, for the loading would take about two days. Christmas was drawing near: greater New York was highly decorated and Santa could be seen in all the stores. I had Christmas dinner at my aunt's house, and she tried to make it look as traditional as she could. She even had the little brown jug on the table. People from the surrounding neighbourhood came to visit. Most of them were fishermen and their wives.

Kathleen came with her friend, but the one I wanted to see most did not put in her appearance. Still, we enjoyed a good Christmas afternoon. One of the men sang a song about a fishing vessel out of Fulton Fish Market in New York called "The *Old Kentucky*." Most of the people who were at my aunt's that afternoon could remember the vessel, and the captain and crew who sailed on her. The ditty seemed to make quite a hit with all the guests, for Mr. Dunn had to sing the song three times that afternoon.

THE *OLD KENTUCKY*

One winter in New York I had a crazy notion,
And I shipped with Captain Jim for to plough the southern ocean,
To get a site with him, I thought I was real lucky
And he was in command of the clipper, Old Kentucky

She was a splendid ship of oak and pine construction
And to ship on board her, they kicked up quite a ruction
She was full-rigged fore and aft some said she was real cranky,
But when she got the wind, she'd outsail the Flying Yankee.

"Now," said Captain Jim, "there's twenty-two of us in here."
Then the cook he rang the bell and we all went down to dinner,
When the meal was through, said he if we are lucky
And if we get the wind we will try the Old Kentucky.

Captain Jim he wore a coat, it was made of pigskin leather
And every time he put it on we'd sure have stormy weather,
Now Captain Jim he knew no fear, he was a real good sailor
And in early days at sea he was skipper on a whaler.

The captain had his crew on deck and all working together,
And right now the Old Kentucky, *she was walking on her weather*
Some of them were smoking pipes, some had them in their faces.
Right then we heard a terrible noise when our main boom broke in
pieces.

When I get back on shore again and clear of the southern ocean,
I will fully understand and no more crazy notions
I will camp her down in old New York and call myself real lucky.
And no more with Captain Jim I'll sail, in the good ship Old Kentucky.

After Christmas was over, I went back to work in the ship. Everyone seemed to be as busy as beavers. The captain came on board and the time was getting close to sail. We found out that we would be sailing on December 28, 1924. As I began to size this ship up, she was becoming more of a mystery to me.

I still didn't like the idea of sailing under sealed orders. A sailor always likes to know on his departure from port the destination of the ship. As I was now signed on, I could not change my mind. So we sailed from New York on December 28.

As we steamed past the Statue of Liberty, the weather was nice and clear, with the cold tang of winter in the air. I was leaving behind my lost sweetheart who had caused me such sorrow, and I knew full well that I could never forget her.

As the *Mermaid* steamed down New York Bay, heading out for the open sea, I took a last look at the Statue of Liberty, with her upraised hand as in farewell. Yes, I was outward bound under sealed orders, and destination unknown on the good ship *Mermaid*.